Northern
Highlands

The author and publisher have made every effort to ensure that the information in this publication is accurate, and accept no responsibility whatsoever for any loss, injury or inconvenience experienced by any person or persons whilst using this book.

published by
pocket mountains ltd
14 Belford Road, Edinburgh EH4 3BL
www.pocketmountains.com

ISBN: 0-9544217-1-X

A catalogue record for this book is available from the British Library

All route maps are based on 1945 Popular Edition Ordnance Survey material and revised from field surveys by Pocket Mountains Ltd, 2001-03. © Pocket Mountains Ltd 2003. Maps on section introduction pages are based on map images © Maps in Minutes™ 2003. © Crown Copyright, Ordnance Survey 2003.

Printed in Poland

Introduction

This guide features forty circular walks in the Northern Highlands. It includes all of the Munros (peaks above 914m/3000ft) and many Corbetts (peaks over 762m/2500ft), as well as other hills that combine to make good circuits.

Routes have been chosen according to a number of factors, including variety of terrain, great views, historical interest, minimal road walking and the feasibility of a circular route.

Environmental factors such as the ability of access points to support additional cars and opportunities for bypassing visitor-sensitive or eroded areas have also been taken into account. Circular routes help to take the pressure off badly eroded paths, and walking in areas where there have been fewer footsteps is more conducive to natural regeneration of the land.

Walkers can also minimise their own impact on the environment by using purpose-built paths whenever possible and walking in single file to help prevent widening scars. Restricting your use of bikes to tracks, parking sensibly, avoiding fires and litter, and keeping dogs on a lead, particularly on grazing land and during lambing, all help to preserve the land and good relations with its inhabitants. Many of the responsibilities for walkers are now enshrined in law.

How to use this guide

The routes in this book are divided into five regions. These divisions largely represent points of access into the mountains, or use natural geographical boundaries. The opening section for each of the five regions introduces the area, its towns, topography and key features, and contains brief route outlines. It is supplemented by a road map, locating the walks.

Each route begins with an introduction identifying the names and heights of significant tops, the relevant Ordnance Survey (OS) map, total distance and average time. Some routes also contain an option for cycling part of the way where there is a long low-level approach.

A sketch map shows the main topographical details of the area and the route. The map is intended only to give the reader an idea of the terrain, and should not be followed for navigation.

Every route has an estimated round-trip time: this is for rough guidance only and should help in planning, especially when daylight hours are limited. In winter or after heavy rain, extra time should also be added for difficulties underfoot.

Risks and how to avoid them

Many of the hills in this guide are remote and craggy, and the weather in Scotland can change suddenly, reducing visibility to several yards. Winter walking brings particular challenges, including limited daylight, white-outs, cornices and avalanches. Every year, walkers and climbers die from falls or hypothermia in the Scottish mountains. Equally, though, overstretched Mountain Rescue teams are often called out to walkers who are simply tired or hungry.

Preparation for a walk should begin well before you set out, and your choice of route should reflect your fitness, the conditions underfoot and the regional weather forecasts. **None of the walks in this guide should be attempted without the relevant OS Map or equivalent at 1:50,000 (or 1:25,000) and a compass.**

Even in summer, warm, waterproof clothing is advisable and footwear that is comfortable and supportive with good grips a must. Don't underestimate how much food and water you need and remember to take any medication required, including reserves in case of illness or delay. Many walkers also carry a whistle, first aid kit and survival bag.

It is a good idea to leave a route description with a friend or relative, in case a genuine emergency arises: you should not rely on a mobile phone to get you out of difficulty. If walking as part of a group, make sure your companions are aware of any medical conditions, such as diabetes, and how to deal with problems that may occur.

There is a route for most levels of fitness in this guide, but it is important to know your limitations. Even for an experienced walker, colds, aches and pains can turn an easy walk into an ordeal.

These routes assume some knowledge of navigation in the hills with use of map and compass, though these skills are not difficult to learn. Use of Global Positioning System (GPS) devices is becoming more common but, while GPS can help pinpoint your location on the map in zero visibility, it cannot tell you where to go next.

Techniques such as scrambling or climbing on rock, snow and ice are required on a number of mountains in this guide. Such skills will improve confidence and the ease with which any route can be completed. They will also help you to avoid or escape potentially dangerous areas if you lose your way. The Mountaineering Council of Scotland provides training and information.

For most of these routes, proficiency in walking and map-reading is sufficient.

Access

Until the Land Reform (Scotland) Act was introduced early in 2003, the 'right to roam' in Scotland was a result of continued negotiations between government bodies, interest groups and landowners.

In many respects, the Act simply reinforces the common law right of access to the countryside of Scotland for recreational purposes. However, a key difference is that under the Act the right of access depends on whether it is exercised responsibly.

Landowners have a legal duty not to put up fences, walls or signs that prevent recreational users from crossing their land, but walkers should also take responsibility for their actions when exercising their right of access. Keep to paths and tracks where possible and, if in doubt, ask. At certain times of the year there are special restrictions, both at low level and on the hills, and these should be respected. Signs are usually posted at popular access points with details: there should be no expectation of a right of access to all places at all times.

The right of access does not extend to use of motor vehicles on private or estate roads.

Seasonal restrictions
Red and Sika deer stalking:
Stags: 1 July to 20 October
Hinds: 21 October to 15 February
Deer may also be culled at other times for welfare reasons. The seasons for Fallow and Roe deer (less common) are also longer. Many estates belong to the Hillphones network which provides advance notice of shoots.
Grouse shooting:
12 August to 10 December
Forestry:
Felling: all year
Planting: November to May
Heather burning:
September to April
Lambing:
March to May (Dogs should be kept on a lead at all times near livestock.)

Glossary
Common Gaelic words found in the text and maps:

abhainn	river
ailean	field; grassy plain
àirigh	summer hill pasture; shieling
allt	burn; stream
àth	ford
bàn	white
beag	small
bealach	pass; gap; gorge
beinn	ben; mountain
bràighe	neck; upper part
cioch	breast; hub; pointed rock
clach	boulder; stone
cnoc	hillock
coire	corrie; cauldron; mountain hollow
creachann	exposed rocky summit
creag	cliff
cruach	heap; stack
dubh	black; dark
garbh	thick; coarse; rough
lagan	hollow; dimple
learg	hillside exposed to sea or sun
lochan	small loch; pool
meall	mound; lump; bunch
mór	big; great; tall
sgòrr	peak; cliff; sharp point
sgùrr	large conical hill
stùc	pinnacle; precipice; steep rock

5

On travelling north and west from Inverness, the rolling farmland of Moray, Cromarty and the Black Isle gives way to the higher terrain of Easter Ross and the Fannich hills. Away from the east coast, the communities are often isolated and the dominant land uses are sheep farming, deer management and forestry.

These mountain routes are all located between Inverness and Ullapool, but they are grouped according to physical geography rather than by points of access. Although the A835 links the boundaries of this region, only two of the routes are accessed directly from the main road.

This section covers three massifs. Ben Wyvis is approached from the Cromarty Firth. The Beinn Dearg massif contains three routes: a long circuit of Beinn Dearg from Braemore; a shorter walk from Inverlael near Ullapool; and a route over Seana Bhraigh from Glen Oykel to the north. There are also three routes in the Fannichs: the

westernmost peaks are taken from the Destitution Road towards Dundonnell; the isolated Fionn Bheinn starts at Achnasheen; and the most arduous route, a traverse of most of the Fannichs, passes the remote shores of Loch Fannich.

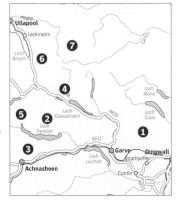

The Beauly Firth to Loch Broom

1   **Ben Wyvis**   8
Long forestry approach to climb several rounded tops with
few paths and some rough terrain

2   **Traverse of the Fannichs**   10
Very long and exhilarating route around a horseshoe of many
peaks. Use of a mountain bike will make access much easier

3   **Achnasheen Terraces**   12
Easily accessible circuit of Fionn Bheinn, with fine views over
the Fannichs. This would make a good half-day outing

4   **Great Wall of Beinn Dearg**   14
Challenging route over several summits at the heart of the massif.
This walk calls for stamina and confidence in route finding

5   **The Western Fannichs**   16
Circuit of A'Chailleach and Sgurr Breac with views into the
corries and a pleasant approach along the glen

6   **Inverlael Forest**   18
Gentle start and good paths through the glen to climb two
peaks close to Beinn Dearg

7   **Strath Mulzie**   20
Long route with some complex terrain between Carn Bàn and
Seana Bhraigh. Use of a mountain bike will help on the approach

Ben Wyvis

Ben Wyvis: Glas Leathad Mór ⓜ (1046m),
Tom a'Chòinnich (953m)

Walk time 7h Height gain 1100m
Approach and return 1h20 bike or 2h20 walk
Distance 20km + 10km approach and return
OS Maps Landranger 20 and 21

**A long route with plenty of rough
riverside walking to follow the graceful
lines of Ben Wyvis. Use of a mountain
bike will reduce access time.**

Start at the turn-off signposted for
Knockmartin just before a telephone kiosk
on the road from Evanton to Loch Glass
(GR569672). (Additional parking over the
bridge.) Cross the bridge, pass the house
and follow the main track which climbs
westwards through the plantation. After
2km, you will come to a junction: take the
minor grassy track to carry straight on
through the trees to a gate. Beyond the
gate, the track climbs west and then
zigzags over open ground to a high point
at another gate. Bikes should be left
here: walk times start from this point
(GR533670). Follow the track down to
the Allt nan Caorach which it keeps
company for 1km before disappearing,
leaving you to continue less easily along
the river towards the main slopes of
Ben Wyvis. After 3km, follow a line of
fenceposts westwards up the steep ridge
to the south of Coire na Feòla: this leads
to a high plateau. From here, it is a much
gentler climb northwest to the main ridge
of Ben Wyvis which leads NNE to the
summit of Glas Leathad Mór (GR463684)
(3h40). The top gives views over the

◀ Ben Wyvis from the Black Isle

wind turbines to the east and the hills of Assynt and Beinn Dearg to the west. Descend northwards to a bealach, and then continue to the top of Tom a'Chòinnich. Drop ENE over ideal running terrain to another bealach, climbing one false summit before ascending the slopes of Meall nan Bradan Leathan (GR493707) (5h40). Descend steepening slopes southeast to Loch Misirich, and then follow the Allt Coire Misirich downstream to reach the main river. Ford the Allt nan Caorach to join the original track which takes you back to the plantation (7h).

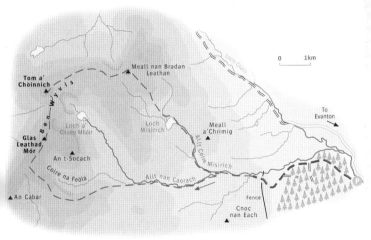

A rare dram

Named after the east coast's highest peak, the original Ben Wyvis Distillery was established at Dingwall in 1879 but, despite being highly regarded by Alfred Barnard on his famous distillery tour of 1887, it was unsuccessful and closed down soon after. Revived by Invergordon Distillers in 1965, this time as part of their large grain complex at Invergordon, it fared no better than its previous incarnation, and the stills were again dismantled at the end of the 1970s. A few bottles of Ben Wyvis have survived from this time, although they are hard to come by and priced accordingly.

Traverse of the Fannichs

An Coileachan ⓜ (923m), **Meall Gorm** ⓜ
(949m), **Beinn Liath Mhór Fannaich** ⓜ
(954m), **Sgurr Mór** ⓜ (1110m), **Meall
a'Chrasgaidh** ⓜ (934m), **Sgurr nan Clach
Geala** ⓜ (1093m), **Sgurr nan Each** ⓜ (923m)

Walk time 8h + detours 1h40
Height gain 1700m
Approach and return 3h bike or 6h walk
Distance 22km + 24km approach and return
OS Map Landranger 20

**An extremely long and challenging
journey over many peaks in a remote
and spectacular setting. A mountain
bike provides the easiest access.**

   Start from the A832, 200m east of
Grudie Power Station at a private road for
the Fannich Estate (GR313625). (Park in the
roadside car park.) Cycle or walk up the
road, gaining height through the trees. After

8km, the dammed loch is reached and the
road turns to gravel before arriving at
Fannich Lodge. Leave bikes close to the
buildings: walk times start from this point.
Head directly up heather slopes in a
northeasterly direction: these lead to the
summit of An Coileachan with its steep
eastern corries (GR241680). Descend
northwest over gentle ground, passing a
shelter just 200m south of the summit of
Meall Gorm (GR222696) (3h). Continue
northwest over undulating ground to the
huge peak of Sgurr Mór. Before the slopes
begin to steepen with small grassy terraces,
take a path which contours across the
southeast face. This leads to the steep east
ridge of the peak with its deep corrie
below. [Detour: Beinn Liath Mhór Fannaich
is on a limb from the main ridge, but also
gives superb views (add 1h).] Climb the east

◀ Beinn Liath Mhór Fannaich from Dirrie More

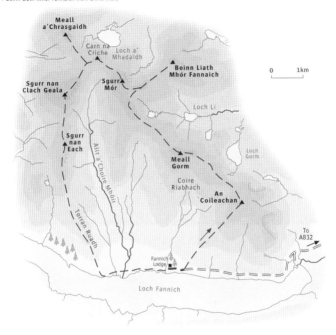

ridge to the scree-laden summit of Sgurr Mór (GR203718) (4h40). Descend west to the flatter ground below Carn na Criche. [Detour: descend northwest to a wide bealach, and then climb to the summit of Meall a'Chrasgaidh. Return the same way (add 40 min).] Bear southwest to begin the ascent of the Am Biachdaich ridge. This climbs steeply by the corrie rim above the Skyscraper Buttress to the curved summit ridge of Sgurr nan Clach Geala (GR185715)

(5h40). From the southern end of the top, descend southwards to a bealach, and then climb a rocky ridge to the pointed summit of Sgurr nan Each with its steep east-facing cliffs (GR184698). Descend to the south, over a knoll, and lose height quickly to reach a plateau before Torran Ruadh. From here, follow the southeast spur to reach a track by the shores of Loch Fannich, which leads to the lodge (8h). Pedal or walk back from here to the main road.

Achnasheen Terraces

Fionn Bheinn ⓜ (933m)

Walk time 4h40 Height gain 800m
Distance 12km
OS Maps Landranger 20 and 25

The reticent peak of Fionn Bheinn has a fine summit corrie and provides great views of Slioch and the Fannichs.

Start from the railway station in the village of Achnasheen (GR163586). Head west to the main road, and turn right to reach a track a short distance away on the opposite side of the road. This leads north, crossing a cattle grid and continuing to a large green barn. Beyond is a field: pass through a gate and along a grassy track. At the top of the field, a gate in the middle of the fence leads to open country. A sunken muddy track climbs steeply over the brow of the hill for some time, before easing slightly over the large area of bog to the west of Creagan nan

The military road to Poolewe

The road from Contin to Poolewe, which passes through Achnasheen, was begun in 1760 by Major William Caulfeild. Poolewe was at this time the main port for the Outer Hebrides, and the road-building strategy was considered important to check potential future rebellions in the Highlands after the Jacobite uprisings. Caulfeild died in 1767 and road maintenance passed into civilian care in 1790, by which time the road had fallen into disrepair. By the turn of the century, it had become impassable by wheeled vehicles.

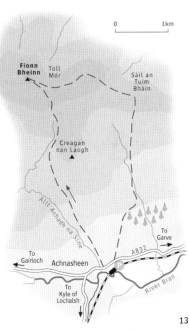

Laogh. When it feels that the track has levelled off, bear northwards up grassy slopes: these lead to the corrie rim and the summit of Fionn Bheinn (GR147621) (2h40). Descend eastwards and follow the edge of the corrie until the ridge starts to turn northeast. Drop east onto Sàil an Tuim Bhàin to reach a wall. From here, descend heather slopes south, aiming for a plantation. After crossing a burn, bear westwards above the plantation to the end of the fence. Now head south over lower grassy slopes to reach one of several exits onto the road. It is a short walk along the road to the station (4h40).

▲ Looking east along Strath Bran

Great Wall of Beinn Dearg

Beinn Dearg ⓜ (1084m), Cona' Mheall ⓜ (978m), Am Faochagach ⓜ (953m)

Walk time 9h Height gain 1400m
Distance 25km OS Map Landranger 20

A long route over many peaks with a good mix of grassy slopes and steep rocky terrain.

Start from the west end of Loch Droma by a dam with a small parking area (GR253755). Cross the road, and pass through the gate to the right of Lochdrum Farm where you will find a burn. Follow this on the west bank to reach a path which rises gently north, and then turns northwest to pass over Meallan Mhurchaidh. Keep to the ridge for another 2km and then turn right at a fork. The path contours around the east side of Beinn Enaiglair until it reaches a series of crags. At this point, descend

north to a bealach and locate another path which zigzags northeast to the top of Iorguill. Descend northeast to join the main west ridge of Beinn Dearg and a wall with its stone vertically stacked like dominoes. Follow the wall eastwards for some distance until you come to an abrupt kink and then leave it to climb south to the summit of Beinn Dearg (GR259812) (4h). Descend north to a different corner of the same wall, and follow it steeply down to a bealach. Curve east around a small mound, and climb scree to the summit of Cona' Mheall. Descend ENE along a rocky ridge, steeply at first and then over complex terrain where slabs try to trick you off the ridgeline. After reaching Loch Prille, climb southeast towards the rounded hill of Meallan Bàn and, beyond, to the summit of Am Faochagach (GR304794) (7h). Descend SSW

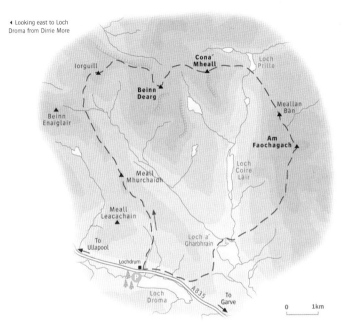

◄ Looking east to Loch Droma from Dirrie More

over gentle terrain and, at a knoll after about 1.5km, bear southwest towards Loch a'Gharbhrain. Pass the loch on its north side (at the water's edge the ground is firm, further north a mass of bog) and climb slightly to gain an old path. Follow this south: it becomes a track and runs parallel to the road back to the start (9h).

Galloway Dykes

Running over the peak of Beinn Dearg is a 'famine wall' built, like the Destitution Roads, in exchange for food by starving labour during the hungry years of the 1840s. Constructed in the traditional 'Galloway' style, these walls were only one stone in width and building them was a highly skilled task as it was difficult to make them stable with no hearting stone in the centre. In many parts, the material used in construction came from the Highlanders' abandoned dwelling-houses.

15

The Western Fannichs

Sgurr Breac (m) (999m),
A'Chailleach (m) (997m)

Walk time 6h20 Height gain 1000m
Distance 17km
OS Maps Landranger 19 and 20

A circuit over two high peaks with dramatic views into the corries.

Start at a track on the west side of a plantation, 5km west of Braemore Junction (GR162761). (Park 100m north of the start point.) Follow the track south beside the trees to a ruin and boathouse by the picturesque Loch a'Bhraoin. Take the boggy path around the foot of the loch, crossing the outlet by a footbridge. Walk SSE by a path to reach the Allt Breabaig and, soon after, ford the river to take a better path.

(When the river is in spate, continue on the west bank.) After a gradual incline for around 4km, the path comes to a bealach in the heart of the Fannichs with views beyond. Bear northwest and climb sharply, avoiding slabs and crags, and passing a steep corrie on the northeast side, to reach the summit of Sgurr Breac (GR158711) (3h40). Follow the ridge westwards around the impressive cirque of Coire Breac and down to a small bealach. Ascend Tomain Coinich and drop down to another bealach (or contour around the top on the south side). Continue westwards along the prominent ridge, with its panoramic views over Loch Toll an Lochain, to the summit of A'Chailleach (GR136714) (4h40). Descend by the NNE ridge for 1km to Sròn na

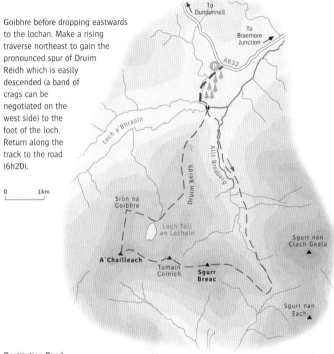

Goibhre before dropping eastwards to the lochan. Make a rising traverse northeast to gain the pronounced spur of Druim Réidh which is easily descended (a band of crags can be negotiated on the west side) to the foot of the loch. Return along the track to the road (6h20).

Destitution Road

Out of several 'Destitution Roads' built in Wester Ross during the 1840s to provide employment during times of famine, the one which runs from Dundonnell at the head of Little Loch Broom to Loch Maree is probably the best known. The relief system was based on the principle that to give assistance to able-bodied Highlanders without demanding work in return was to encourage 'moral degradation'. According to Lowland opinion of the time, 'the great cause of the destitution is not the failure of the potato crop but the intense and abominable idleness of the inhabitants.'

◀ Leitir Fhearna and Coire Breac

17

Inverlael Forest

Meall nan Ceapraichean ⓜ (977m),
Eididh nan Clach Geala ⓜ (927m)

Walk time 7h40 Height gain 1100m
Distance 22km OS Map Landranger 20

This route passes beneath Beinn Dearg's imposing western ridge to climb two peaks by good paths.

Start from the track by the phone box on the A835 at Inverlael (GR183853). (Park tightly along the old road, leaving access for farm vehicles.) Walk east along the track into Inverlael Forest, keeping to the south bank of the River Lael until you reach a bridge near Glensguaib. Cross over, and continue eastwards on the track: this leaves the plantation as a path after about 1km, and the dark cliffs of Beinn Dearg come into view. After a while, the path passes a series of waterfalls. Ignore a left turning just after the falls, and continue by the path as it steepens beneath the cliffs. The terrain

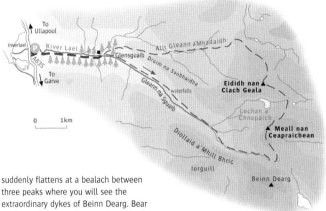

suddenly flattens at a bealach between three peaks where you will see the extraordinary dykes of Beinn Dearg. Bear easily northwest to the summit of Meall nan Ceapraichean (GR257825) (4h20). Contour around to the north peak, and descend northeastwards to another bealach with a small lochan. Climb northwest over easy slopes to the summit of Eididh nan Clach Geala (GR257842) (5h20). Drop down to the north, and keep to the flatter ground before rising gently to some boulders. Descend WNW off the hill. You will soon join an excellent path which follows the Allt Gleann a'Mhadaidh before crossing it to join the ridge of Druim na Saobhaidhe. The path rapidly loses height and passes through a gate to enter woodland. Switchbacks lead through the plantation to Glensguaib, leaving only a short walk back to the start (7h40).

The Hector People

It is thought that more than 170 men, women and children boarded the old Dutch ship, the *Hector*, at Loch Broom on 8 July 1773 to set sail for new lives on the Pictou Plantation in Nova Scotia. Smallpox and dysentery took their toll, and at least eighteen children died at sea. By the time the rotting hulk landed, people were picking at the planks to find worms to eat. It is estimated that there are more than 140,000 descendants of the 'Hector People' living in Canada and the United States today.

◀ Strone Nea from the River Lael

Strath Mulzie

Carn Bàn ⓒ (845m),
Seana Bhraigh Ⓜ (927m)

Walk time 6h40 + detour 40 min
Height gain 1200m
Approach and return 3h20 bike
Distance 19km + 30km approach and return
OS Maps Landranger 16 and 20

**A strenuous route into remote country.
Use of a mountain bike is advised for
the approach.**

Start from the Oykel Bridge Hotel on
the A837 (GR384008). (Park just south
of the new bridge on a small road that leads
south.) Continue along this road and past
a row of peach-coloured cottages:
soon after, the road turns to gravel and

crosses the river by a bridge. Follow the
main track westwards as it gains altitude
above the glen and then drops down to an
old farmstead at Duag Bridge. Bear south
towards Corriemulzie Lodge (GR323951).
After passing farm buildings, the track
comes to a gate. Beyond this, the
spectacular cliffs of Seana Bhraigh come
into view. Continue along the track until
you come to some large stepping stones
across the river after about 5km. Leave
bikes here: walk times are given from this
point. Cross the river, and climb south
along the track to a small cottage by the
side of Loch a'Choire Mhóir. From here,
climb east up fairly steep terrain, aiming for
a crag on the hillside, and then follow the

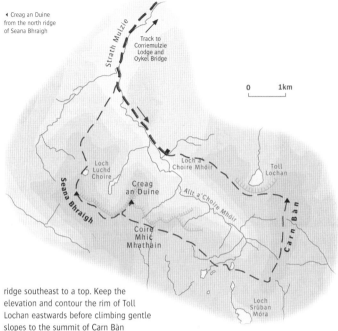

◀ Creag an Duine
from the north ridge
of Seana Bhraigh

ridge southeast to a top. Keep the elevation and contour the rim of Toll Lochan eastwards before climbing gentle slopes to the summit of Carn Bàn (GR338876) (3h). Now bearing south, follow the ridgeline to the southernmost top which has the best views of the distant hills of Assynt, then drop WNW into a complex terrain of bog and slabs to find a triangular-shaped loch. Maintain the same direction across difficult country for 2.5km: there are steep cliffs if you stray too far north. This leads eventually to Coire Mhic Mhathain and another lochan. Climb WNW to reach a bealach between Seana Bhraigh and Creag an Duine. [Detour: follow the exposed ridge of this spectacular subsidiary to its top (some brief scrambling) before returning to the bealach (40 min).] Climb southwest over a smaller top and then northwest to the summit of Seana Bhraigh (GR281879) (5h40). Take care at this point as there are cliffs: when starting the descent, a small detour southwards is necessary to avoid a steep gap. Descend NNE to a flat area with a lochan. Drop northwards to reach gentler ground leading back to the track (6h40). Return the same way to Oykel Bridge.

Referred to by Alfred Wainwright as the 'last great wilderness', this area is arguably the remotest and most undisturbed in Britain. The great estates of Dundonnell, Fisherfield and Letterewe are noted for their exceptional natural beauty, with deep lochs, waterfalls and rocky peaks. Long approaches and returns, tricky navigation and high cliffs make mountain skills essential for many of these walks.

In this section, the road between Dundonnell and Poolewe gives access to four routes: a difficult traverse of An Teallach; long approaches to Mullach Coire and Fisherfield Forest; and an easy but no less scenic ascent of Beinn Ghobhlach. To the south, between Gairloch and Kinlochewe, there are also four routes. The peaks of Flowerdale and the easier circuit of Meall a'Ghiubhais are in Torridon but accessed from Loch Maree. Slioch is approached from Kinlochewe. A route from

the far shore of Loch Maree leads through the Letterewe Estate, home to the remotest mountains of all.

Dundonnell to Kinlochewe

1 **The An Teallach Ridge**   24
Challenging route on an exposed ridge with many towers negotiated
by scrambling and abseils. Mountaineering experience a must

2 **The Mullach Coire Massif**   26
Remote setting for a long route over multiple tops. A river crossing
early on in the circuit may at times prove difficult

3 **Lochans of Beinn Ghobhlach**   28
Relatively short walk along the loch shore to reach a quiet peak
with water all around

4 **Fisherfield Forest**   30
Varied route in remote country. A long trek in to climb Beinn Dearg
Mór and two other peaks, with some steep and exposed sections

5 **Peaks of Flowerdale**   32
Entertaining circuit of Beinn an Eòin and Baosbheinn. This includes
steep sections, particularly in descent, and some tricky route finding

6 **Dark Lochs of Letterewe**   34
An extended trek over Ruadh Stac Mór and Á Mhaighdean, Britain's
remotest hills. The long approach makes this an ideal two-day walk

7 **Meall a′Ghiubhais by the mountain trail**   36
Short, steep route in the Beinn Eighe National Nature Reserve, with
excellent access paths and views of the Torridonian peaks

8 **Slioch**   38
Popular mountain horseshoe, with a gentle approach and return along
the river. Good paths and one section of awkward descent

The An Teallach Ridge

An Teallach: **Bidein a'Ghlas Thuill** ⓜ
(1062m), **Sgurr Fiòna** ⓜ (1060m),
Sàil Liath (954m)

Walk time 8h Height gain 1300m
Distance 17km OS Map Explorer 435

**A spectacular ridge walk for seasoned
mountaineers, with mandatory
scrambling, severe exposure and
recommended abseils. The route is
particularly serious in winter.**

Start at the signposted turning for
Badrallach, 3km south of Dundonnell
(GR113856). (Park just south of the house
of Corrie Hallie.) Walk 400m north along
the road until you reach a gate on the right
and a burn (which passes under the road)
on the left. Turn left onto a path on the
north side of the burn. This path, marked
with posts (although occasionally hard to
see) follows the water south through
rhododendron and Scots pine, and out into
open country. Continue on the north side
for about 1km to a neat waterfall. Follow

the smaller burn westwards until the banks
steepen, and then bear southwest over
broken sandstone terraces towards Glas
Mheall Liath and its impressive north-facing
cliffs. Climb straight up the east ridge
where easy terraces and outcrops give way
to small boulders before the summit (3h).
After a flat, rocky section, the ridge leads
you to a series of towers which can be
scrambled (the exposure on the north side
is extreme, a taster for the main ridge to
come) or else bypassed on the southern
side to reach the summit of Bidein a'Ghlas
Thuill (GR068844). Descend with ease
along the southwest ridge to a bealach and
climb to the summit of Sgurr Fiòna: the
angle is steep, but there are no difficulties.
The next 500m of the southeast ridge is
serious: consider roping up for this section
unless very confident. Descend from the
top and up over Lord Berkeley's Seat with
its overhanging tower. The four pinnacles of
Corrag Bhuidhe come next. They require
careful traversing and descent, keeping to

◂ An Teallach from Fain, between Braemore and Dundonnell

the west side as you lose height. The second pinnacle may require a short abseil of 5-10m, and the fourth has a very steep drop and an abseil of 20m may be preferable to help reach safer ground. [Variant: the exposure can be lessened by skirting around the pinnacles on the southwest side, but care is still required.] After this point,

progress is much easier: continue over Cadha Gobhlach and to Sàil Liath, the final top (GR072825) (6h20). Descend southeastwards for 1.5km to reach an excellent track. Follow this northeast and back to the road (8h).

An Teallach Ale

An Teallach Ale is produced at the Orr family croft at Camusnagaul, just west of Dundonnell, in their fully manual microbrewery. With a strength of 4.2%, the An Teallach is a dark ale whereas the Beinn Dearg, which they also produce, is a reddish, lighter beer at 3.8%. Beer aficionados and walkers are welcome to visit and sample the ales.

The Mullach Coire Massif

Beinn a'Chlaidheimh  (916m),
Sgurr Bàn (989m), **Mullach Coire
Mhic Fhearchair** (1018m),
Beinn Tarsuinn (937m)

Walk time 11h Height gain 1600m
Distance 33km OS Map Landranger 19

**A long traverse of a remote massif, with
a river crossing. Good cyclists might
consider a mountain bike for the
approach, although this does not save
much time.**

Start just south of Corrie Hallie, about
600m south of the turning for Dundonnell
House and Badrallach on the A832
(GR114851). A rocky gorse-flanked track on
the west side of the road leads south
through a gate and thereafter follows the
Allt Gleann Chaorachain, crossing it after

2km to zigzag up to a plateau. Continue
along the track into the picturesque Strath
na Sealga to reach a small plantation after
7km. At this point, ford the Abhainn Loch an
Nid (this may prove difficult when the river
is in spate) and climb the heathery slopes
of Creag Glas on the vague northeast ridge
of Beinn a'Chlaidheimh. The final 300m is
steeper but the summit ridge with its
several tops is soon reached (GR061775)
(4h20). Drop south to a flat area and climb
or pass a knoll before descending to Am
Briseadh above a circular loch. The huge
rocky slopes of Sgurr Bàn lead easily to its
summit. Descend southwest to a bealach
before tackling the final 200m of Mullach
Coire Mhic Fhearchair, the highest peak in
the massif (GR052735) (6h20). Drop south
towards the subsidiary peak of Meall Garbh.

◄ The massif of Mullach Coire from An Teallach

A sneaky path contours under its steep northwest face to reach Bealach Odhar. Climb grassy slopes WNW to the summit of Beinn Tarsuinn: it is worth the extra effort for the views north along Gleann na Muice. Descend southeast to a burn, and then bear eastwards over undulating terrain to reach the well-hidden Bealach na Croise. Keep to a path above the north side of the burn. This eventually reaches Loch an Nid where it joins a better path on the east

side of the glen. Follow this for 5km to the plantation and along the track to the road (11h).

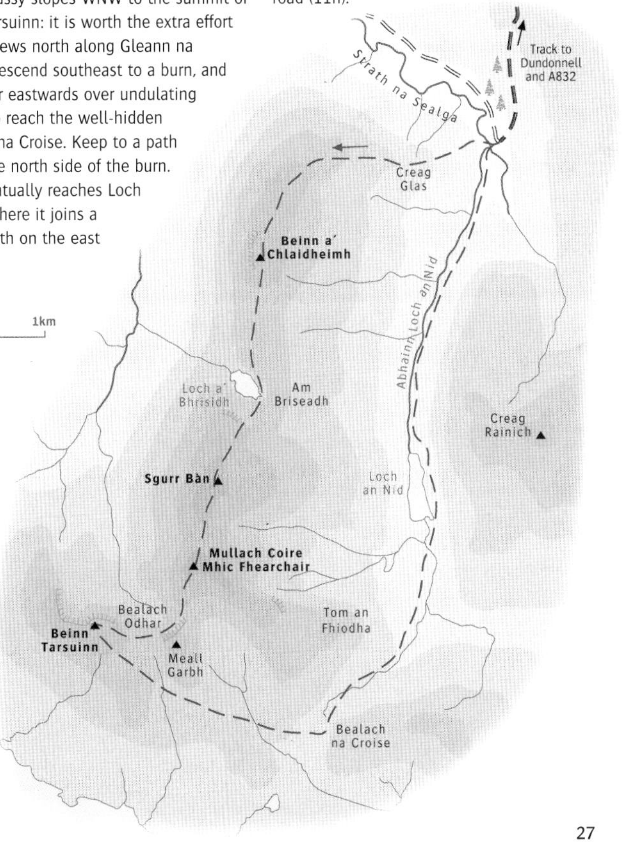

Track to Dundonnell and A832

Strath na Sealga

Creag Glas

Beinn a' Chlaidheimh

Abhainn Loch an Nid

0   1km

Loch a' Bhrisidh

Am Briseadh

Creag Rainich

Sgurr Bàn

Loch an Nid

Mullach Coire Mhic Fhearchair

Bealach Odhar

Tom an Fhiodha

Beinn Tarsuinn

Meall Garbh

Bealach na Croise

Lochans of Beinn Ghobhlach

Beinn Ghobhlach (635m)

Walk time 4h Height gain 600m
Distance 9km OS Map Landranger 19

An ascent of a modest peak on the peninsula between Loch Broom and Little Loch Broom.

Start at the end of the road at Badrallach 1km beyond the campsite (GR056918). (Limited parking here.) Take the path, which follows the loch shore westwards and then northwards under cliffs towards the isolated village of Scoraig. After crossing an obvious burn (which flows from Loch na h-Uidhe) after about 3km, leave the path and follow the burn steeply east. This enters a bowl beneath two bands of cliffs: exit left along a gully to view the main peak of Beinn Ghobhlach. Walk northeast over boggy ground for a short distance and gain the terraced southwest ridge of Beinn Ghobhlach. This takes you past small

sandstone crags and up to the summit (GR056943) (3h). Descend eastwards for about 500m in distance to avoid cliffs, and then drop down to Loch a'Bhealaich. Follow the burn westwards to the larger Loch na Coireig. Walk around to the south side of the loch, and then climb steeply southwards to find a pair of small lochans. Descend grassy slopes southeastwards, crossing a burn to return to your start point (4h).

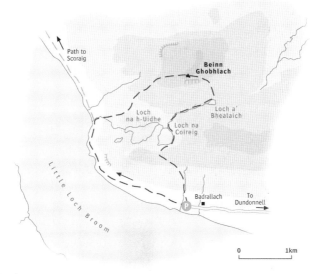

Scoraig

The small vibrant community on the Scoraig peninsula on the north side of Little Loch Broom is one of the more unusual in northern Scotland. Despite being offered an access road by the council, the self-reliant inhabitants prefer to cross the loch or walk miles to get to and from their homes. Similarly, they have no need for a mains electricity supply as their houses are powered by batteries charged from small but very efficient wind turbines built by hand in Scoraig.

◀ Beinn Ghobhlach from Ardmair

Fisherfield Forest

Creag-mheall Mór (628m), **Beinn Dearg Mór** Ⓒ (910m), **Beinn Dearg Bheag** Ⓒ (820m)

Walk time 8h Height gain 1600m
Approach and return 1h40 bike or 4h walk
Distance 20km + 12km approach and return
OS Map Landranger 19

An unorthodox circuit of some remote peaks, with several steep sections of ascent and descent. Use of a mountain bike will reduce access time. In winter this becomes a serious undertaking.

Start by the roadbridge over the Gruinard River, midway between Poolewe and Dundonnell on the A832 (GR962912). (Limited parking by the bridge.) Take a good track on the west side of the river: this leads southwards up the glen. The track passes through a small plantation and eventually descends to a plain, where there is a concrete bridge over the Allt Loch Ghiubhsachain by an old ruin. Bikes should

be left here: walk times are given from this point. Bear SSW to begin the climb over steep slopes: these lead to a featureless area of bog with a gentle incline. Continue south to ascend the rocky knoll of Creag na Sgoinne. The ridge becomes much more defined further up: follow it to Creag-mheall Mór, and descend to the calming Lochan na Bearta. Climb SSE to regain the ridge, which drops to the main path from Letterewe to Dundonnell. Keep to the path for the short distance to Loch Beinn Dearg, and follow the northeast shoreline until you are about midway. From here, ascend the steep southwest slopes of Beinn Dearg Mór: an old wall leads you for part of the way. It is a long climb, but you will eventually come to a series of broken crags below the summit ridge. The reward for negotiating these is the impressive view along the vertical towers of the southeast spur. Continue north to the summit (GR032799)

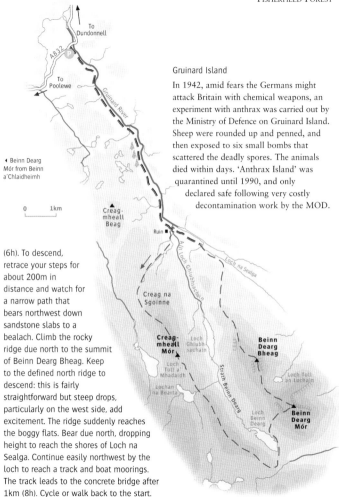

To
Dundonnell

A832

To
Poolewe

Gruinard River

◄ Beinn Dearg
Mór from Beinn
a'Chlaidheimh

0   1km

Creag-
mheall
Beag

Ruin ■

Allt Loch Ghiubhsachain

Loch na Sealga

Gruinard Island

In 1942, amid fears the Germans might
attack Britain with chemical weapons, an
experiment with anthrax was carried out by
the Ministry of Defence on Gruinard Island.
Sheep were rounded up and penned, and
then exposed to six small bombs that
scattered the deadly spores. The animals
died within days. 'Anthrax Island' was
quarantined until 1990, and only
declared safe following very costly
decontamination work by the MOD.

Creag na
Sgoinne

**Creag-
mheall
Mór**

Loch
Ghiubh-
sachain

Loch
Toll a'
Mhadaidh

Lochan
na Bearta

Strath Beinn Dearg

**Beinn
Dearg
Bheag**

Loch Toll
an Lochain

Loch
Beinn
Dearg

**Beinn
Dearg
Mór**

(6h). To descend,
retrace your steps for
about 200m in
distance and watch for
a narrow path that
bears northwest down
sandstone slabs to a
bealach. Climb the rocky
ridge due north to the summit
of Beinn Dearg Bheag. Keep
to the defined north ridge to
descend: this is fairly
straightforward but steep drops,
particularly on the west side, add
excitement. The ridge suddenly reaches
the boggy flats. Bear due north, dropping
height to reach the shores of Loch na
Sealga. Continue easily northwest by the
loch to reach a track and boat moorings.
The track leads to the concrete bridge after
1km (8h). Cycle or walk back to the start.

Peaks of Flowerdale

Beinn an Eòin ● (855m),
Baosbheinn ● (875m)

Walk time 8h40 Height gain 1400m
Distance 24km OS Map Landranger 19

**A strenuous circuit with some steep
ground in descent that makes it
particularly challenging in winter
conditions. The route affords great
views over the Torridonian peaks.**

Start at a big green shed east of Loch Bad
an Sgalaig (GR857721) on the A832. (Park
here, leaving access.) A track on the
opposite side of the road leads southeast,
crosses a bridge and passes through a gate
into the Gairloch Estate. Follow the track
over a bealach and along the Abhainn
a'Gharbh Choire. After about 5km, you will
come to some stepping stones across a
burn and, beyond this, the track rises

bringing Loch na h-Oidhche into view. At a
large square boulder on the left, bear east
across moorland towards the ridgeline of
Beinn an Eòin. Keep to the north side of the
cliffs and follow a small burn over
sandstone terraces to attain the ridge.
Follow the ridge SSE over small knolls
before the final ascent to the summit of
Beinn an Eòin (GR905646) (4h). Descend by
the south ridge: this is rocky and steep in
places, requiring care. About halfway down,
there are some crags: these are best
circumvented on the western side to reach
Pòca Buidhe, a stalking lodge (GR899644).
Bear west between the lochans and over
bog, and begin climbing towards the
southeast ridge of Baosbheinn. Climb to the
top of Ceann Beag with its striking
hexagonal block. Descend to a small
bealach and continue northwards over

interesting terrain to another minor top. Drop again before starting the sustained climb to the grassy summit of Baosbheinn (GR870654) (6h20). Follow the northwest ridge down over two towers, which require careful descent as there are steep cliffs to the west. Bear north across the undulating plateau. Just beyond a knoll and before a large cairn and overhanging rock, begin your descent over a steep grassy slope on the northeast side to meet a burn that flows north. Follow it downstream over rough terrain to reach a deer fence. Cross this using the rungs on either side of the burn and, keeping height, bear northeast over heather to join the Abhainn a'Gharbh Choire. Cross this by a bridge and head north across bog, aiming for a small grassy bealach. Climb over this, dropping down the far side to reach the original track. It is 2km back to the start point (8h40).

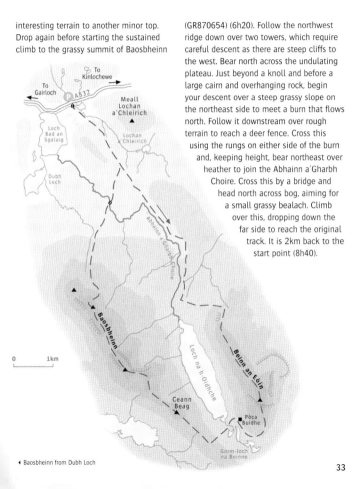

◀ Baosbheinn from Dubh Loch

33

Dark Lochs of Letterewe

Ruadh Stac Mór ⓜ(918m),
Á Mhaighdean ⓜ(967m)

Walk time 9h20 Height gain 1600m
Approach and return from Kinlochewe
along Loch Maree (13km one way)
or from Poolewe via Kernsary, starting the
route from Carnmore (also 13km one way)
or direct across the loch by boat or canoe
Distance 26km OS Map Landranger 19

**A demanding circuit over remote peaks
and around crags and deep lochs. This
terrain is amongst the wildest in Britain.**

Start from Letterewe on the north shore of
Loch Maree (GR953713). About 150m
northeast of the turreted white lodge, there
is a smaller house with a gate on its right.
This leads to a path which begins to climb
steeply through shrubbery, crosses the Allt
Folais by a footbridge and climbs to
Bealach Mhèinnidh. The path then starts to
zigzag down to Fionn Loch, which lies in

front of the spectacular Carn Mór crags. At a
fork just before the loch, turn left to cross
the spiked causeway to the house at
Carnmore. Continue east under Sgurr na
Laocainn, rising steadily to join the Allt
Bruthach an Easain. Walk northeast through
the hanging valley until just over the
bealach: watch for a path that heads
southeast around the foot of a lochan. This
crosses the moorland and leads south of the
screes of Ruadh Stac Mór. Soon this path
starts to climb steeply east to the ridge. The summit of Ruadh Stac Mór
is just beyond (GR018756) (5h20). About
10m south of the trig point, a narrow path
picks its way through rocks, descending
sharply southeast. Lower down, you must
breach a set of low crags to reach the
bealach. From here, rejoin the first path to
climb the slopes of Á Mhaighdean to the
summit. Descend SSE down easy grassy
slopes. Lower down the terrain becomes

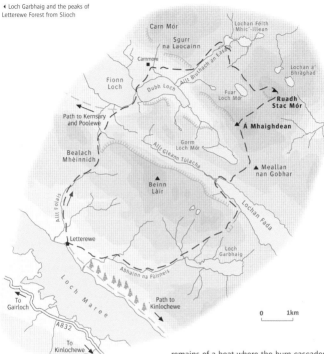

◀ Loch Garbhaig and the peaks of Letterewe Forest from Slioch

0   1km

more complex: keep to the west of Meallan nan Gobhar, to cross the ridge of Beinn Tharsuinn Chaol. Negotiate steep awkward slopes southwards to reach the narrow Lochan Fada, and walk around the head of the loch. From here, follow the southwest shore of the loch by a small path. After about 1.5km, this leads to the upturned remains of a boat where the burn cascades over slabs. An old path zigzags southwest on the north side of a burn. This is hard to find, but becomes more defined as it climbs to a bealach with a low set of crags. From here, it is downhill all of the way: bear WSW along a good path to pass close to Loch Garbhaig, and then follow the Abhainn na Fùirneis to reach a track in the trees. This leads back to Letterewe (9h20).

Meall a'Ghiubhais by the mountain trail

Meall a'Ghiubhais Ⓒ (887m)

Walk time 4h Height gain 900m
Distance 8km OS Map Explorer 433

A varied and part-waymarked route giving great views over Beinn Eighe and along Loch Maree.

Begin at the Beinn Eighe National Nature Reserve car park and information point (GR001650). Walk under the low roadbridge close to the information shelter and immediately fork left, following the mountain trail. This is a well-built path which climbs south through differently marked zones as old forest gives way to exposed crags, and eventually reaches the top of an outcrop with a good panorama of Beinn Eighe (GR993634) (1h40). Continue on the path, which drops to the northwest and wanders through level but rocky terrain. Just after a small lochan on the left, the path turns north. [Escape: follow the path as it descends to the north and back to the start.] Leave the path here, and bear westwards up gradually steepening slopes. These eventually lead to the north peak of Meall a'Ghiubhais: it is a short walk southwest to the true summit (GR976634) (3h). From the low point between the two tops, descend NNW for 500m to avoid cliffs and then follow a vague ridge northeast. Where the terrain flattens out, bear

southeast to a small loch, then descend by a burn to join the path. This trail leads northwards, hugging the west bank of a deep ravine before dropping below the treeline. At a junction, turn right. This brings you back to the start (4h).

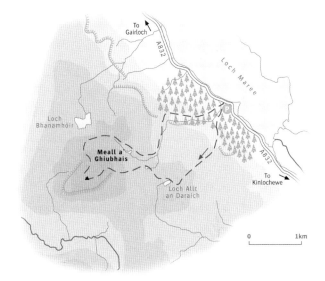

The furnaces of Loch Maree

Sir George Hay, a wealthy lawyer, came to Loch Maree in 1607 after his business partner was executed for treason. He built a furnace on the north shore near Letterewe to take advantage of the bog iron in the hills and the dense forest around the loch. An Act of Parliament in 1609 prohibited the use of natural Scottish woodland, but Hay was able to gain an exclusion, granted by King James VI, which permitted him to log, mine and smelt until 1643. He began similar operations in other local areas, imported ore from Lancashire and hired miners from Cumbria. Hay made himself a fortune, but removed most of the native forestry in the process.

◀ The forests of Meall a'Ghiubhais and Beinn Eighe beyond

Slioch

Sgurr Dubh (738m), **Slioch** Ⓜ (981m),
Sgurr an Tuill Bhàin (934m)

Walk time 7h Height gain 1000m
Distance 19km OS Map Landranger 19

**A horseshoe circuit of a popular
mountain which overlooks Loch Maree
and the wild Letterewe Forest.**

Start from the car park at the end of
Incheril, just east of Kinlochewe
(GR037624). Exit by a gate on the north
side of the car park and follow a track,
which soon turns to a rough path,
westwards along the fence. Continue
northwest along the Kinlochewe River: the
path has several variants but all arrive close
to the shores of Loch Maree after about
4km. Cross the Abhainn an Fhasaigh by a
footbridge, and start to climb northeast by a
path which leads away from the river. This
has a gentle initial climb, but steepens as
you approach Coire na Sleaghaich. Where
the trail flattens near Meall Each, leave the
path to ascend the steep western slopes of
Sgurr Dubh which lead directly to the top.
From here, follow the northwest ridge,

climbing over a knoll before descending to a lochan (GR012682). [Variant: instead of climbing Sgurr Dubh, continue into the corrie towards the main peak of Slioch for 1km and then climb sharply west to reach the lochan.] Ascend the steep and sandy southeast ridge of Slioch which leads to a plateau, after which it is only a short distance to the double summit (GR004688) (4h). Drop eastwards along a narrowing ridge before rising to the top of Sgurr an Tuill Bhàin. Descend south into Coire na Sleaghaich. Before reaching the knoll of Meall Each, follow a burn which begins to drop steeply southeast. The terrain is a little awkward, but the path along the idyllic Gleann Bianasdail is soon reached. Continue to follow the river and its many small waterfalls to the bridge, and then follow the Kinlochewe River back to the start (7h).

Mourie and Maelrubha

Loch Maree and one of its islands, Eilean Maree, are thought to be named after the Irish Saint Maelrubha, who founded a Christian community at Applecross in the 7th century. It was a sacred place to locals before Christianity arrived, however. The Moon deity *Mourie* was honoured with the sacrifice of animals (usually bulls), and it later became the custom to take the insane to the island as it was believed that by dunking them in the loch and making them drink water from a sacred well they would be cured.

◀ Slioch and Loch Maree

In 1877, Queen Victoria visited Glen Torridon and was amazed by the landscape which she described in her diary as 'grand, wild, savage-looking, but most beautiful and picturesque'.

The Torridonian sandstone towers and pinnacles that impressed the Victorians remain a major attraction for walkers and climbers. The peaks are all steep-sided bastions, requiring stamina, technique and confidence.

The area is known for the diversity of its flora, and is protected by two organisations. The National Trust for Scotland owns much of the north side of the glen, while Scottish Natural Heritage manages the Beinn Eighe National Nature Reserve which overlooks Loch Maree.

This section includes five routes that are reached from Glen Torridon: the western half of the Beinn Eighe massif; the Liathach and Beinn Alligin traverses; and the less climbed peaks of Beinn Dearg and Beinn Damh. Another route on Beinn Eighe starts

from Kinlochewe. To the south, three routes from the road between Shieldaig and Lochcarron are also featured: one takes in the vast corries of Beinn Bhàn; and two begin north of the River Carron to climb the peaks on the south side of Glen Torridon.

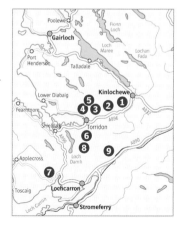

Torridon

1 **Slabs and pinnacles of Beinn Eighe**   42
Challenging horseshoe over a varied landscape. This route involves
considerable exposure, and scrambling skills are required

2 **Triple Buttress**   44
Great circuit of a mountaineering classic, with steep grassy slopes
to ascend and a short section of easy scrambling

3 **Liathach**   46
Entertaining and exposed ridge with steep ascent and descent.
Scrambling is optional, but will add to the excitement of this route

4 **The Horns of Beinn Alligin**   48
Popular circuit of a mountain whose towers and cliffs have given it
legendary status. Scrambling skills will help on trickier sections

5 **Beinn Dearg at the heart of Torridon**   50
Traverse of a less known peak with panoramic views. Good access
paths, but some exposure higher up and a steep descent to the glen

6 **Beinn Damh**   52
Fine ridge walk with a long approach through the glen. Some rough
terrain in descent, with an entertaining return along the old road

7 **Corries and cliffs of Applecross**   54
Winding route over the wild peak of Beinn Bhàn which provides
some exposure and a good test of navigation skills

8 **The Red Slabs**   56
Rocky circuit of Maol Chean-dearg and An Ruadh-stac, accessed by
a good path. Rough terrain and scrambling add to the adventure

9 **Fuar Tholl and Coire Làir**   58
Excellent ridge walk over three peaks. Good paths to start, but some
exposure and complex terrain higher up

Slabs and pinnacles of Beinn Eighe

**Beinn Eighe: Ruadh-stac Beag ⓒ (896m),
Spidean Coire nan Clach ⓜ (993m),
Sgurr Bàn (970m), Sgurr nan Fhir
Duibhe (963m)**

Walk time 7h40 Height gain 1200m
Distance 15km OS Map Explorer 433

**A circuit on the Beinn Eighe massif with
many sections of tricky scrambling.
The slabs on Spidean Coire nan Clach
and the pinnacles known as the Black
Carls make this a serious route in
winter conditions.**

Start from the Beinn Eighe Visitor Centre
at Aultroy, 1km north of Kinlochewe
(GR020630). Follow the green mountain
signs for the Upper Ridge Trail. This
leads westwards out of the trees, across a
bridge and along a burn. At a fork, continue
westwards along a path by the water,
gaining altitude steadily. At another
junction below a gate, continue west
along the glen and cross a stile. The path
fades when it reaches a plateau and a series
of cairns, which combine to form a strange
moonscape. Leave the plateau in a
southwesterly direction, losing some height
to ford the Allt Toll a'Ghiubhais. Aim
directly for the broad east face of Ruadh-
stac Beag and look for a series of caves just
left of centre. Climb scree here to reach
smooth rocks, which can be easily

scrambled. One tricky step is encountered before easy terraces lead rightwards onto the ridge. Continue south to the summit (GR973614) (3h20). Drop southwards over terraces to more scree: this makes for an awkward descent to flatter ground. Keep to the east side of the ridge below the lochan, and aim for a short gully. Climb up alongside it to reach vast slabs on the east side of Spidean Coire nan Clach. These provide excellent scrambling, though difficult when wet, and lead to a point just short of the summit (GR966597). Descend eastwards along a prominent ridge, and over towers to the top of Sgurr Bàn. Drop steeply east past the northern corrie, a

cathedral of organ pipes and scree, and then climb to the summit of Sgurr nan Fhir Duibhe (GR981600) (5h40). The jagged pinnacles of the Black Carls on the north ridge provide the final scrambling: the harder sections are best avoided on the east side, apart from the final two drops which should be taken on the west. The ground then undulates to Creag Dhubh, the last point on the ridge. Descend a good path to reach the east ridge. Further down, at a knoll with a cairn, drop north into a corrie. From here, the path follows the Allt a'Chuirn, crossing a burn and deer fences before reaching the road. This leads back to the start via Kinlochewe (7h40).

◀ The eastern half of the Beinn Eighe massif from Meall a'Ghiubhais

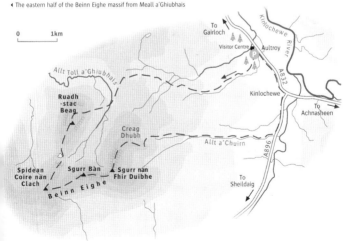

43

Triple Buttress

Beinn Eighe: **Còinneach Mhór** (976m),
Ruadh-stac Mór ⓜ (1010m),
Spidean Coire nan Clach ⓜ (993m)

Walk time 6h + detour 1h
Height gain 1000m
Distance 17km OS Map Explorer 433

For mountaineers, the name 'Triple Buttress' is synonymous with the exposure, isolation and geological interest of the Northern Highlands.

Start from the car park near the Ling Hut, midway between Torridon and Kinlochewe (GR957568). The path by the bridge follows the Allt a'Coire Dhuibh Mhóir north, gaining steady height until it passes beneath the flanks of Liathach, after which it flattens out. Cross the river by some stepping stones, and continue upstream. The path forks at a cairn: take the path on the right which rises north and then east to circumnavigate Sàil Mhór, before reaching two waterfalls. Climb alongside the burn to arrive at the flat sandstone terrace by Loch Coire Mhic Fhearchair: here, the Triple Buttress comes into view. Walk clockwise around the loch, where you might come across the remains of a light aircraft. Climb southwestwards over grass between Sàil Mhór and the Triple Buttress. This is easier than it looks, and only steepens once the ridge is attained. Bear eastwards and scramble up the exposed ridge (difficulties can be minimised by keeping on the south side) to the flat and grassy summit of Còinneach Mhór (GR944601) (4h). Continue

east to the end of the summit ridge. [Detour: drop down the north ridge to a bealach, and then climb gently to the summit of Ruadh-stac Mór. Return the same way (add 1h).] Descend southeast to a bealach, and climb eastwards to the trig point below Spidean Coire nan Clach. The true summit is a short climb to the northeast. Return to the trig point.

Drop south over switchbacks for 300m in distance to a cairn. At this point, turn off the ridge to drop steeply east into Coire an Laoigh. A good path leads down to a small plantation and the road. Walk west to the start (6h).

Mountaineering in the Northern Highlands

With over 40 routes on the Triple Buttress alone, Beinn Eighe attracts many climbers. Only a few people have developed new routes in hills like Beinn Eighe, Beinn Bhàn and Liathach since the 1970s. These include Martin Moran and Andy Nisbet, both locals, and Mick Fowler, who used to drive up from London almost every weekend in winter. The Triple Buttress not only has three linked towers, it is also made up of several layers: a base of Lewisean Gneiss, a sandstone core and a crown of quartzite.

◀ The Triple Buttress from Coire Mhic Fhearchair

45

Liathach

Liathach: **Stùc a'Choire Dhuibh Bhig**
(915m), **Spidean a Choire Léith** ⓜ
(1055m), **Mullach an Rathain** ⓜ(1023m)

Walk time 7h Height gain 1100m
Distance 10km OS Map Explorer 433

**A classic ridge walk in an exciting and
exposed position high above Glen
Torridon. Scrambling skills will make
this expedition even more rewarding. In
winter, the route is a serious undertaking.**

Start by two long passing bays at a
kink in the A896, about 500m east of a

plantation and Glen Cottage (GR936565).
A new path leads from the eastern passing
bay and climbs steeply north by the Allt an
Doire Ghairbh. Higher up, the path enters
the rocky amphitheatre of Coire Liath Mhór.
Keep east of the burn and a deep chasm:
the path climbs steeply over sandstone
blocks to reach the top of the ridge. (To
climb Stùc a'Choire Dhuibh Bhig, descend a
little to the east and climb easily to the
top, returning the same way.) Climb west
over three rocky pyramids: these can be
ascended without too much difficulty to

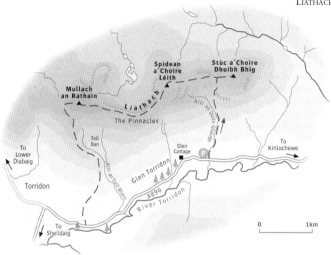

begin the last long haul to the summit of Spidean a'Choire Léith (GR929579) (3h). Descend to the southwest, following a path through scree. This keeps corrie-side to avoid steeper ground, before traversing back to the ridge at a notch which marks the start of the pinnacles. The many needles, steps and rock buttresses provide entertainment, but tricky points can be bypassed on the southern flanks if required. Eventually the terrain eases, and it is a

long, gentle climb to the summit of Mullach an Rathain (GR912577) (5h20). Descend southwest for 200m in distance, and follow the prominent southeast ridge. This overlooks the screes of Toll Ban, and drops sharply through occasional rock bands. Further down, descend to join the Allt an Tuill Bhain which can be followed for a while by a good path. The path leaves the burn and emerges at the road between two small plantations. Walk back up the road to the start (7h).

The Golden Cave

The making of illicit whisky and the avoidance of the exciseman was a favourite pastime for many in Torridon. One of the best known and elusive caves connected with the manufacture and smuggling of *uisge beatha* is known as the Golden Cave, close to the road at the foot of Liathach. The cave is around 20ft deep and named after a streak of yellow lichen in the rock or, according to some, because it once concealed a horde of gold belonging to Bonnie Prince Charlie, hidden during the time of the 1745 Jacobite Rising.

◀ Liathach and the village of Torridon from the east

The Horns of Beinn Alligin

Beinn Alligin: **Na Rathanan** (866m),
Sgùrr Mhór ⓜ (986m),
Tom na Gruagaich ⓜ (922m)

Walk time 6h Height gain 1200m
Distance 10km OS Map Explorer 433

**A great horseshoe with some exposure
and optional scrambling. The route is a
serious proposition in winter.**

Start at the car park where the road to
Diabaig crosses the Abhainn Coire Mhic
Nòbuil (GR869576). Take the path which
leads northeast along the south bank of the
river. After 2km, cross the river by a bridge
and continue north by a good path (ignoring
the path that branches to the right after
200m). Climb alongside the Allt

a'Bhealaich, cross by a bridge and continue
on the opposite bank until the path forks at
a cairn 800m beyond the first bridge. Take
the path on the left which bears northwest
towards the steep buttress of Na Rathanan
(the Horns). Climb the northeast spur by a
giant's staircase of sandstone blocks to
reach the Horns of Alligin. The best line
scrambles over the top of all three Horns
but requires careful climbing and descent,
particularly when icy. All tricky sections can
be avoided, however, by following an
exposed path worn in the grass slopes on
the south side. Beyond the Horns, the climb
west to the summit of Sgùrr Mhór is steep
but uncomplicated (GR865613) (4h). Care is
needed as you start to descend: close to the

◄ Afternoon mist on Sgùrr Mhór near the Black Notch

summit the cleft of Eag Dhubh, or Black Notch, splits the mountain on its south side, so bear westwards for 100m before descending southwest to the safety of the next bealach. After a small knoll to the southwest, the final rocky ridge of Tom na Gruagaich involves an exposed climb to the summit (GR859602). To descend from the ridge, bear 100m west to a small bealach where a cairn marks the start of a path. Follow this steeply through Coir nan Laogh, keeping company with various burns, and then south across moorland to the start point (6h).

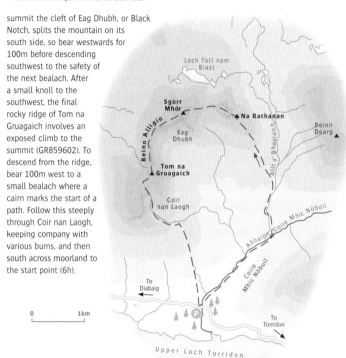

The Black Notch

The great gash which splits Beinn Alligin's main summit, Sgùrr Mhór, in half is known locally as the Black Notch of the Outcry. This was formed by a massive landslide, the debris of which can still be seen in the corrie below. Legend has it that shepherds often heard inexplicable shouting from here until one day a man fell to his death and the cries stopped.

Beinn Dearg at the heart of Torridon

Beinn Dearg C (914m)

Walk time 6h40 Height gain 1000m
Distance 17km OS Map Explorer 433

An exciting but less popular traverse with spectacular views of the Torridonian peaks. This route entails one exposed section and a steep descent.

Start at the car park where the road to Diabaig crosses the Abhainn Coire Mhic Nòbuil (GR869576). Take the path which leads northeast along the south bank of the river. After 2km, cross the river by a bridge, bear north for about 200m and take the right fork where the path splits. Follow the river eastwards between Beinn Dearg to the north and the buttresses and corries of Liathach to the south. When you reach the watershed by Loch Grobaig (GR922597), leave the path and climb northwest, keeping to the high ground. The terrain steepens, but soon leads to the top of Carn na Feòla with its high point on the north side (GR915613) (3h20). Descend slightly along the west ridge to a bealach with eroded sandstone bedding planes. The tower to the northwest, which should be taken on its southern side, provides an exposed traverse. From here, the ridge continues easily but with interest to the summit of Beinn Dearg (GR895608) (5h). Drop northwest along a well-defined ridge and climb to Stùc Loch na Cabhaig. Descend the northwest ridge: this is steep and rocky at first, but becomes easier with a

path most of the way. Lower down, the ridge loses definition: heather and rocks lead steeply down to the wide basin of the Allt a'Bhealaich. Cross to the far side of the glen, and climb a short distance to join a path running south. Further down, the path crosses to the east bank by a wooden bridge and soon meets the original intersection. Cross the Abhainn Coire Mhic Nòbuil and follow it back to the start (6h40).

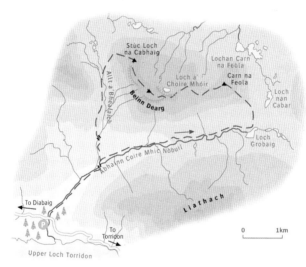

The Diana Legend

In the pass between Beinn Dearg and Beinn Alligin, cattle raiders from Gairloch ran into another party, which included a woman called Diana, from Loch Carron. With only one bull from Loch Carron as their spoil, they decided to equally share the meat before going their separate ways. It was soon noticed, however, that the beast's liver was gone. Accusations were made, and all but one of the men were slain in the course of the dispute. He saw Diana run off clutching the meat and so gave chase, killing her at the crest of the pass. The spot was marked by a small cairn erected by her kinsfolk.

‹ From the summit of Beinn Dearg with Liathach and Beinn Eighe beyond

Beinn Damh

Beinn Damh Ⓖ (903m)

Walk time 6h Height gain 1000m
Distance 15km
OS Maps Landranger 24 and 25

A varied ridge and shoreline walk, with some adventure and great views. The route involves an awkward descent from the final peak, which can be avoided.

Start from the bridge over the Allt Coire Roill, close to Ben Damph Lodge (GR887540). (Park by the bridge or in Annat.) Walk west along the road for about 100m to locate a good forest path on the left. This climbs steadily through rhododendron, with glimpses of a high waterfall from between the trees. At the last of the stunted pine, the path forks: take the path on the left which leads to the river. Walk upstream to cross the river where it is

fordable and then double back to join the path which now continues SSE, rising very gently over moorland for 3km. At the bealach of Drochaid Coire Roill, there is a lochan with views of Maol Chean-dearg. Trend southwest along the short ridge: this entails some easy scrambling, which can be avoided by keeping to the north side and later gaining height. The ridge reaches a flat area below the rounded northeast ridge of Spidean Coir an Laoigh. Cross the corrie under high crags to reach the more pronounced east ridge of the peak. This is steep but never too difficult, flattening out for 50m before the final rocky buttress which marks the highest summit of Beinn Damh (GR893502) (3h20). Descend northwest to a bealach, and then continue over rounded terrain to the north summit.

◂ Beinn Damh from the lower slopes of Beinn Alligin

Drop west and then northwest above Toll Bàn. [Escape: take a path to the northeast, which leads back to the waterfall.] Climb Meall Gorm and Sgurr na Bana Mhoraire beyond (GR870527). Descend northwest: this can be tricky as the terrain is rough, with rocky steps to negotiate or avoid. Further down, the ground levels out by a lochan before dropping steeply west to the private road (signposted for Torridon Smolts Ltd). Follow this to the A896, and cross here to pass between two buildings. The track behind is the old road: follow it east to reach the inlet of Ob Gorm Mór with its fabulous views of Beinn Alligin. East of the inlet, the trail becomes obscured by twisted branches. After 2km, it emerges at Ben Damph Lodge (6h).

The Rhododendron

Scotland is home to about 1000 non-native species of flora and fauna. One of the most prevalent alien plants is the rhododendron (*Rhododendron ponticum*), introduced from more temperate regions. The plant grows invasively in forested areas, crowds out less dominant native species and blocks the light to understorey plants: they are considered a serious nuisance on the west coast, and prove hard to remove.

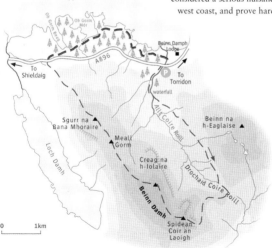

Corries and cliffs of Applecross

Beinn Bhàn C (895m)

Walk time 6h20 Height gain 900m
Distance 16km OS Map Landranger 24

A route which weaves a complex passage through spectacular cliffs. Navigation over the tops can be difficult in winter or poor weather conditions.

Start by a bridge over the River Kishorn 400m west of Tornapress (GR834423). (Park on the east side of the bridge.) A good path leads north from the bridge, gaining gradual height before coming to a small footbridge after 2km. At this point, leave the main path and follow a vague trail on the south side of the burn towards the cliffs of Beinn Bhàn. At a large boulder, cross the burn and continue northwest, passing another boulder, before reaching Lochan Coire na Poite beneath the imposing cliffs of A'Phoit and A'Chioch. Continue northwest into the

wild arena of Coir' an Fhamair. Straight ahead, there are steep grassy slopes: climb these, keeping left of two rock needles and a boulder field, to reach the plateau. Bear southwards and follow the high ground – watching for cliffs to the east side of the ridge and the occasional deep hole – to the summit of Beinn Bhàn (GR803450) (4h). To descend, follow a twisting spur WSW: the path, which leads to Bealach nan Arr, can be easily lost. From the bealach, descend south by a steep grassy ramp. This soon eases, bringing you into another cirque. To descend, follow the Allt Coire nan Arr on its north side to the flatter, boggy terrain below the towering cliffs of Sgurr a'Chaorachain. Eventually you will come to the Loch Coire nan Arr: keep to the east bank to reach the foot of the loch where a track leads to the road. Walk east along the road to the start (6h20).

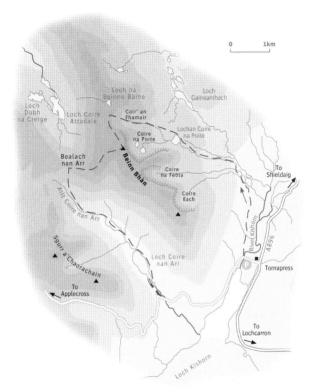

Bealach-nam-Ba

The steep and narrow road out to Applecross village from the head of Loch Kishorn is called *Bealach-nam-Ba*, Pass of the Cattle, and was once the main way through for cattle being driven to the markets in the east. At its highest the road is 625m (2053ft) above sea level, and the sharp hairpin bends and breathtaking views have earned it a reputation as the most prominent pass in Scotland. As it was not built for the modern car (or caravan), passing can at times be difficult and it is not a journey for the faint-hearted, especially on misty days.

◄ Beinn Bhàn from the east

The Red Slabs

Maol Chean-dearg ⓜ (933m),
An Ruadh-stac ⓒ (892m)

Walk time 5h40 + detour 1h20
Height gain 900m
Distance 15km OS Map Landranger 25

**A varied route with some easy
scrambling above the unusual Coire an
Ruadh-stac and its multi-tiered lochans.**

   Start from a bridge over the Fionn-
abhainn just west of Coulags (GR957451).
(Park 50m west of the bridge.) Walk north
along the farm track for 200m, and then
follow the signs for Glen Torridon towards
the river to avoid the lodge. A good path
climbs gently along the east bank of the
river before coming to a bridge after 2km.

Cross the bridge and continue to gain
gradual height up the glen, past the bothy
of Coire Fionnaraich and to a fork in the
path. Take the path on the left, which winds
west up to Bealach a Choire Gharbh
(GR932488). [Detour: ascend the southeast
ridge of Maol Chean-dearg over a steep
rocky knoll. The terrain flattens before a
final sharp climb to the summit and its
princely seating arrangement (GR924499).
Retrace your steps to the bealach (add
1h20).] Bear southwest across the complex
boulders and shelves around the rim of
the corrie to reach a bealach between
Meall nan Ceapairean and An Ruadh-stac.
Scramble southwest over worn slabs,
keeping to the ridge. Beyond the slabs,

the route continues with interest to the summit of An Ruadh-stac (GR922481) (3h40). Descend south to reach the uneven terrain around Ruadh Stac Bheag, and follow the easier ground southwestwards. Where the slopes start to ease to the south, drop towards Meall an Daimh and a lochan over boggy ground. Descend ENE under the flanks of Ruadh Stac Bheag to reach the more northerly of two burns, and follow this east to Loch Moin a'Chriathair. Follow the north bank of the outlet from here, dropping gently at first and then sharply at a series of waterfalls. Where the burn flows down a ramp, leave its banks to traverse easily ENE. Cross a boulder field to the original footbridge, and return to the start (5h40).

Strome Castle

Strome Castle by Loch Carron was built in the 15th century and came into the possession of the Macdonalds of Glengarry in 1539. It was besieged many times by their rivals, including Kenneth MacKenzie of Kintail in 1602. He had been about to give up when a prisoner who had escaped from the Macdonalds informed him that he had heard some women being scolded for spilling water on the ammunition store. With the enemy seemingly disarmed, MacKenzie offered safe passage to the inhabitants for the surrender of the castle. They accepted and the stronghold was blown up, never to be rebuilt.

◄ Strome Castle with Skye in the distance

Fuar Tholl and Coire Làir

Fuar Tholl Ⓒ (907m), **Sgorr Ruadh** Ⓜ (962m), **Beinn Liath Mhór** Ⓜ (926m)

Walk time 7h40 Height gain 1600m
Distance 16km OS Map Landranger 25

A challenging circuit around a large corrie, with two rocky peaks on the outward journey and a long quartzite ridge to return. This is a serious route to attempt in winter.

Start at the turn-off for Achnashellach Station in Strath Carron (GR003484). (Roadside parking.) Walk up to the station, cross the line and pass through a gate. Climb a track to a fork after about 100m. Turn left onto a forestry track and follow this for about 500m, then take the signposted path down to and along the River Làir. This soon leaves the river and rises over switchbacks to the rim of the corrie before branching. Turn left again to cross the river: this may be difficult when it is in spate. Zigzag gently towards Fuar Tholl. As the terrain steepens, the corrie cliffs come into view. When you reach the edge of the corrie and can see the lochan, leave the path and climb the north spur. This is steep at first but soon relents, with some clambering over large sandstone boulders to reach the summit (GR975489) (3h). Descend southwest to a bealach, and climb to the second top above the Mainnrichean Buttress. Drop southwest, with care, to a notch. From here, it is clear why the crag has been a favourite with climbers. Descend steeply northwest on a

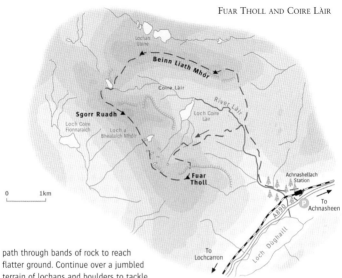

path through bands of rock to reach flatter ground. Continue over a jumbled terrain of lochans and boulders to tackle the broad south slopes of Sgorr Ruadh: these lead eventually to the summit (GR959505). Descend northwest along the ridge to a point beyond a large quartzite scar where the terrain rises again. Drop east to a secluded lochan and path. [Escape: follow this path east back through Coire Làir.] Ignore the path and ascend a knoll to the northeast: this is steep, with short, avoidable buttresses. After dropping slightly, continue to climb northeast to the

westernmost and highest summit of Beinn Liath Mhór (GR964519) (5h40). Follow this excellent ridge east over 2km of shattered quartzite to the central and eastern tops. From the latter, descend ESE along a small path: this is not too difficult at first, but you should later keep east to avoid cliffs. This joins a good trail back to the edge of the corrie. Return on the original path to Achnashellach (7h40).

The railway to Kyle of Lochalsh

The railway craze had reached the Highlands by the mid-19th century, and Inverness was connected to the south by 1858 with a route through Aberdeen. A few years later, the engineer Joseph Mitchell proposed a line to Skye via Kyle of Lochalsh to compete with the existing ferries, encourage tourism and transport fish, sheep and cattle to the markets. The Dingwall and Skye Company was beset by financial problems, and initially the line was only complete as far as Strome. The last part to Kyle was finally opened in 1897.

◄ Coire Làir with Fuar Tholl and Sgorr Ruadh

The hills of Assynt were, according to legend, thrown down by Norse Gods as a prelude to bigger projects. It is not hard to see how this story came about: the shapes of these hills have a mesmeric quality quite unlike anything else in Scotland. Stac Pollaidh, Quinag and Suilven are not so high in altitude, but they are striking in the way that they rise suddenly from the moor like humpbacked creatures emerging from the sea. The area is famous for its geology, glaciology and weathering: academics and school groups come here from all over the country to study the rocks and strata.

Most of the routes in this section are accessed from the A835 between Ullapool and Scourie: this includes the twin routes on the peaks of Cùl Mór and Cùl Beag; the hidden gems of Glas Bheinn; and the natural fortress of Quinag. Coigach and Stac Pollaidh are approached from the road for Achiltibuie. Glen Oykel, to the east of

Ledmore, is the base for a serious walk over Ben More Assynt, the region's highest peak. Lochinver is the start point for a climb on Suilven, which is arguably Assynt's most charismatic peak.

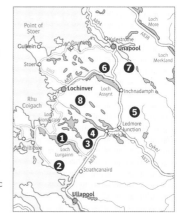

The Hills of Assynt

1 **Stac Pollaidh**   62
Short climb up an iconic peak. Scrambling skills are needed to gain the highest point

2 **The Seven Peaks of Coigach**   64
Multi-topped horseshoe with an exhilarating finish along a sharp, exposed ridge and a steep descent

3 **Cùl Beag and Inverpolly Reserve**   66
Short off-path circuit on a wild peak with great views. This route involves some steep sections of ascent and descent

4 **Cùl Mór from Knockan Crag**   68
A compact route in an area rich in geology. Good access paths and a steep climb over boulders make for a varied circuit

5 **Ben More Assynt by Glen Oykel**   70
Arduous walk with a fair bit of exposure over Assynt's highest peaks. Some scrambling, with the hardest in descent. A bike will ease access

6 **Pipes of Quinag**   72
Short route over a complex fortress with an initial steep ascent over scree and an easy descent from the final peak

7 **Waterfalls and lochans of Glas Bheinn**   74
Fairly short walk by interesting paths. This circuit involves one steep ascent and occasional route finding difficulties in rough terrain

8 **Suilven the Hypnotic**   76
Long route over a captivating peak with a short, sharp climb and some adventure on return

Stac Pollaidh

Stac Pollaidh (613m)

Walk time 3h Height gain 600m
Distance 6km OS Map Explorer 439

**A short but exciting walk up a
photogenic peak. Scrambling is required
for the highest point, but any part of the
summit ridge is worth the climb.**

Start south of the mountain at the
parking area and information point on the
route to Achiltibuie, 8km from the A835
(GR108095). Pass through a gate to head
northwards up the renovated path. This
divides just before a fence: take the left fork
through a gate. The trail traverses the
western side of the mountain, rising gently
beneath sheer cliffs that provide some of
the best rock climbing in the north. Keep to
the most prominent path, which now climbs
the north side of the peak. Before reaching
a fence, climb steeply eastwards by large
steps to reach the blocks and towers of the
summit ridge. The easiest tower is a simple
walk to the east, returning the same way.

To reach the highest point on the ridge, an exciting scramble through a rocky labyrinth is required. To get there bear west, keeping to the south side of the first tower, then scramble up a gully and cross the apex. Continue by a path on the north side, passing rock needles: an awkward step leads to the last tower but one. Some scrambling is required to reach the final buttress, but really any tower on the arête constitutes an ascent (2h). Return to the point where you ascended the ridge and drop northeast by a good path, keeping to the east side of the fenced area. When it reaches gentler ground, this path leads clockwise to the south face of the mountain. Pass through the gate to reach the road (3h).

Weathering

The ice age was responsible for shaping the mountains in this area, but more recent weather has also taken its toll. The freeze-thaw process during the winter is brought about by the shift in temperatures when wet and warming influences such as the Gulf Stream alternate rapidly with colder weather events, such as winds arriving from Scandinavia. This is an efficient way of physically breaking down huge boulders and crags into smaller cobbles and pebbles. Water seeps into nooks and crannies and, on freezing, expands to exert pressure on the rocks: this process is repeated many times until the rocks crumble. Much of the scree to be found on the tops is formed in this way.

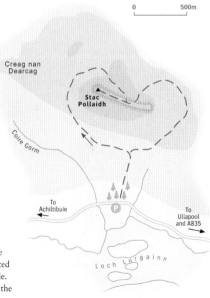

◄ Stac Pollaidh from the southeast

The Seven Peaks of Coigach

Cairn Conmheall (541m), **Beinn nan Caorach** (649m), Unnamed (648m), **Sgùrr an Fhidhleir** (703m), **Speicein Còinnich** (717m), **Ben Mór Coigach** (743m), **Garbh Choireachan** (733m)

Walk time 5h20 Height gain 1000m
Distance 12km OS Map Landranger 15

An entertaining walk over many rocky tops with great views out to the Summer Isles and an exposed ridge to finish.

Start at the highest point on the road just before Culnacraig (GR061043). (Park in the layby here or back towards Achiltibuie.) Head northeastwards across bog to climb steepening slopes. After a while, veer north aiming for the summit of Cairn Conmheall (GR065055). Drop eastwards to a bealach, and take the steep west ridge of Beinn nan Caorach. Once on the top, follow the ridge northeast, descending over barren ground before climbing to a knoll with its views of Stac Pollaidh and the near vertical north buttress of Sgùrr an Fhidhleir. Descend south and climb the slopes of the Fhidhleir to its summit (GR094954) (2h40). To avoid steep cliffs, drop southwest for about 300m

in distance and then continue southeast over the bealach, before climbing Speicein Còinnich. The summit is an independent top set some distance from the eastern side of the plateau. Double back and follow the ridge west towards the rounded Ben Mór Coigach. From here, the twin tops of Garbh Choireachan are reached along a knife-edge arête, with optional scrambling. Descend

the west ridge until you reach the point where the rocks crumble into talus, and then bear northwest over heather to the Allt nan Coisiche. Cross this above a ravine, and then follow a small path. Maintain height and traverse northwest until another path is joined just before the Allt a'Choire Réidh. Return to the road at Culnacraig (5h20).

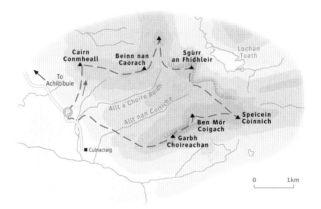

The Summer Isles

The Summer Isles, consisting of Tanera Mór, Tanera Beag and a couple of dozen smaller islands have not been permanently inhabited since 1931, although around 120 people still lived on Tanera Mór in 1881. Tanera Mór is the only Scottish island to operate a private postal service, and the *MV. Patricia* regularly crosses the Sound of Badentarbat to pick up and drop off the post at Achiltibuie. The island has also issued its own very collectible stamps since 1970, some of which feature images of the birds found on nearby Priest Island and Isle Martin, both RSPB sanctuaries.

◄ Garbh Choireachan from Ardmair

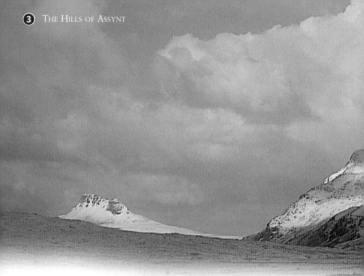

Cùl Beag and Inverpolly Reserve

Cùl Beag Ⓒ (769m)

Walk time 4h Height gain 600m
Distance 11km OS Map Landranger 15

A short route with some steep climbing rewarded by views over Inverpolly. The peak is smaller but has a wilder countenance than Cùl Mór.

   Start from the upper of two parking areas about 1km south of Knockan Crag Visitor Centre (GR184078). Follow the remains of an old tarmac road, which loops from the west side of the A835. After 200m, a path leads west across moor and zigzags down to Loch nan Ealachan and some fencing. The path ends abruptly here, but continue west to climb the ridgeline of Creag Dhubh: this becomes more defined as it levels off. Ascend the steep east face, which is easier than it looks, to reach the top of Meall Dearg. Descend west over sandstone slabs to a lochan. The east face of Cùl Beag is

A man in Assynt

Much of the work of Edinburgh poet Norman MacCaig (1910-1996) featured the natural environment of Scotland, the people of rural communities, and their relationships with the landscape and each other. 'A man in Assynt', his longest and one of the best known poems, follows the history of the mountains he loved from their prehistoric formation to the Clearances and beyond. His *Collected Poems* are published by Chatto Poetry.

also steep, but soon leads to the summit (GR140088) (2h40). Drop southwards to join another steep ridge, avoiding the cliffs on the west side. Where the terrain eases, head for the Allt Leathad Doire Ruaidhe.

Cross the burn to follow its north side until level with the foot of Meall Dearg, and then bear ENE across bog to reach the original path at Loch nan Ealachan which leads back to the road (4h).

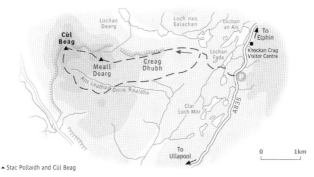

▲ Stac Pollaidh and Cùl Beag

67

Cùl Mór from Knockan Crag

Cùl Mór Ⓖ (849m)

Walk time 4h20 Height gain 700m
Distance 11km OS Map Landranger 15

A popular and accessible mountain with good views over the lochs and peaks of Inverpolly.

Start at a parking bay 300m north of the Knockan Crag Visitor Centre (GR188094). Pass through a gate, and bear north on a renovated path which gains altitude slowly. The path fades out when you reach the ridge of Meallan Diomhain, but this can be ascended without difficulty westwards to the top of the knoll. Descend gently to the northwest to attain the north ridge of Cùl Mór with its small lochan hidden in a dip. Ascend the ridge over the sandstone boulders of its east side to reach the summit (GR162119) (2h40). Drop down over rocky outcrops and grass to a bealach. From here, climb southeast to the top of Creag nan Calman, which gives the best views of Stac Pollaidh and Inverpolly. Descend the east ridge and, where the terrain eases, head east into

a corrie. Bear eastwards to cross the burn and reach a lochan, and then continue east across undulating and boggy ground to reach the path at the foot of Meallan Diomhain. This leads directly back to the start (4h20).

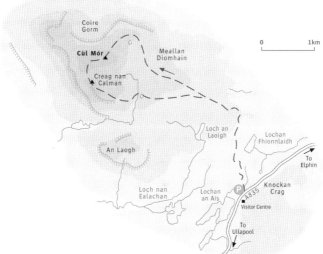

The great debate

The early days of geology were strongly influenced by the belief that the world was created in six days: to claim otherwise was heresy. Rocks and mountains were thought to be formed only in catastrophic events and not from the slow processes we understand today. Early Victorian geologists also believed mountains were formed by the vertical movement of the earth's crust. The concept of horizontal forces detaching and moving large slices of crust along low-angled faults was a theory that had been aired some years earlier in Europe, originally to much derision from the scientific community. It was not until detailed study of the Moine Thrust that these new ideas gained wider acceptance. The interactive visitor centre at Knockan Crag is a good place to find out more about Assynt's geology.

◀ Inverpolly from Cùl Mór

Ben More Assynt by Glen Oykel

Ben More Assynt (998m),
Conival (987m)

Walk time 6h20 Height gain 1000m
Approach and return 1h20 bike or 3h walk
Distance 17km + 12km approach and return
OS Map Landranger 15

**Two high peaks taken by a narrow ridge
to form a remote and technical route.
This involves some scrambling and a
steep and exposed descent. It would be
a serious undertaking in winter.**

   Start at a forestry track 200m west of
Badger's Lodge and 4km southeast of
Altnacealgach Motel (GR296083). Walk or
cycle northeast up the track (access is
restricted to walkers and cyclists), which
drops to cross the glen and pass Benmore
Lodge. Beyond the lodge and by another
house, go through a gate: the track turns to

gravel and follows the River Oykel
northwards to reach a gate at the edge of a
plantation. Mountain bikes are best left
here: walk times are given from this point.
Beyond the gate, cross the Allt Sail an
Ruathair by a footbridge and follow a track
north along the River Oykel. The trail soon
fades but an old path continues north, rising
above the east side of the glen to pass two
shielings. Before reaching the buttress
ahead, climb northeast up steep grass
slopes to an area of bog which hides Dubh
Loch Beag. On the far side of the loch,
ascend steeper grass slopes to a rounded
bealach north of Eagle Rock. Follow the
southeast ridge of Carn nan Conbhairean to
its top and twin cairns. From this point,
there are steep slopes and cliffs on each
side as the great ridge begins. Descend
north, with care, to a bealach. Climb to a

top and onwards to the summit of Ben More Assynt with its two shattered pyramids (GR318201) (4h). From this point, the ridge undulates westwards over sharp quartzite blocks and boulders, dropping to a bealach before rising to the summit of Conival. Drop SSE along a prominent ridge: its towers and buttresses make for an exciting descent but, despite being very exposed, this requires only brief scrambling and a good head for heights. Where the terrain eases, head due south into Glen Oykel and follow the river over boggy ground for about 2km. After passing a small waterfall, trend southeast to reach the original path. Retrace your steps to the track and the edge of the forest (6h20). Cycle or walk back to the start.

Ardvreck Castle

Once the stronghold of the MacLeods of Assynt, the castle on Loch Assynt was built around 1590 and is principally known for being the temporary home of James Graham, the 1st Marquis of Montrose. He spent time in the dungeons here in 1650 after being betrayed to the Covenanters following the Battle of Carbisdale near Bonar Bridge. The charismatic Marquis had inspired great loyalty among his Highland followers, and his betrayal at the castle went against all clan custom. Sentenced to death without trial in Edinburgh, he was hanged and disembowelled before a mob silenced by his composure on the gallows.

◀ Conival from Loch Assynt

Pipes of Quinag

Quinag: **Sàil Gharbh** ⓒ (808m),
Sàil Gorm ⓒ (776m),
Spidean Còinich ⓒ (764m)

Walk time 4h + detour 1h20
Height gain 800m
Distance 10km OS Map Landranger 15

A short route over a complex massif with imposing cliffs. The line of ascent can be hard going.

Start from a large parking area which faces the east flank of Spidean Còinich (GR233274). Almost directly opposite, a good path leads northwestwards across boggy ground into the very heart of the corrie. Walk around Lochan Bealach Cornaidh until you are about halfway along the north shore and then climb due north over slopes of grass and sandstone boulders, a fairly tough section which gains height quickly. This eventually comes to the main ridge a short distance from the summit of Sàil Gharbh (GR209292) (2h20). Descend westwards to a small bealach and rise to a top at the centre of the Quinag massif. This point gives the best view of the northeast face of Spidean Còinich. [Detour: descend north to climb a tower and

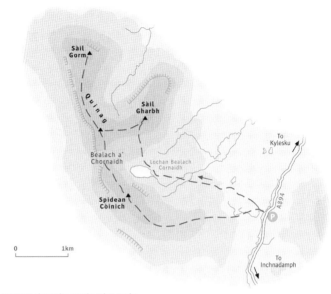

continue along the gentle ridge to the top of Sàil Gorm. Return the same way (add 1h20).] Descend steeply south by a path that keeps to the corrie side to Bealach a'Chornaidh, and then climb southwards to the top of a knoll. Drop again to a tiny lochan on a plateau before one

last steep ascent, this time to the summit of Spidean Còinich (GR205277) (3h20). Descend southeast onto flat quartzite slabs of pipe rock. The broad east ridge of the mountain leads back to the road (4h).

Pipe rock

Pipe rock is composed of vertical columns between 3 and 15mm in diameter and up to 1m long. From the surface, a cross-section of pipe rock looks like white pockmarks or shallow circular indentations. Once under the ocean, the 'pipes' in this sandstone rock were created by worm-like creatures called *Skolithus* which tunnelled deep into the sediment. Their burrows then filled with sand. The rock is more than 550 million years old and has been folded and thrusted at later periods. More recently, in the ice ages, the mountains were sculpted and scoured by glaciers, but these fossil burrows are still visible today.

◀ Quinag from Duartmore Forest

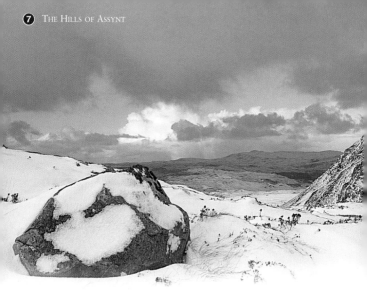

Waterfalls and lochans of Glas Bheinn

Glas Bheinn ⓒ (776m)

Walk time 4h40 Height gain 800m
Distance 12km OS Map Landranger 15

A winding walk through magnificent terrain. A short detour gives views over Eas a Chùal Aluinn, the highest waterfall in Britain.

Start from a parking spot by a hairpin bend at the foot of Loch na Gainmhich (GR240292). Walk southwards along the road: after 300m, a path cuts through the heather on the left. Follow this due south and continue straight on at an intersection. A grassy ramp descends from the north ridge of Glas Bheinn: here, a steep climb by a path takes you to the main ridge which is followed more easily with views over the many lochans and buttresses of this peak. Skirt the edge of the cirque around Loch a'Choire Dheirg to reach the summit (GR255265) (2h). Follow the ridgeline southwest for 600m in distance to the point where a sharp spur drops east to a bealach shared with Beinn Uidhe. A path descends north and begins to navigate the wildly undulating terrain, forcing you eastwards to eventually meet a rocky basin containing a lochan (GR280270). The path branches at this point: take the left fork to descend northwest to another lochan. To detour to

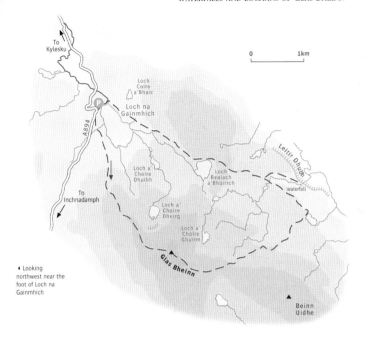

◀ Looking northwest near the foot of Loch na Gainmhich

the top of the waterfall, follow a burn eastwards to the point where the Chùal Aluinn plunges out of sight. Return to the main path before climbing west for 1km until the ground flattens and the Loch Bealach a'Bhùirich comes into view.
The path follows the shoreline, and drops gently to the north of Loch na Gainmhich. Ford the foot of the loch and find the road beyond (4h40).

The Assynt Crofters

The Assynt Crofters' Trust was formed in 1992 by about 100 crofters in order to raise funds to purchase the North Lochinver Estate from a bankrupt Swedish property developer. Money came from many public and private sources, including individuals whose ancestors had been evicted from the land during the Clearances. It was a major turning point in the land reforms of the Highlands, and other communities have followed their lead. The estate is now run by a board of crofters democratically elected in each of the 13 townships.

Suilven the Hypnotic

Suilven: Caisteal Liath (731m),
Meall Meadhonach (723m)

Walk time 7h40 + detour 1h
Height gain 800m
Distance 23km OS Map Landranger 15

**The charismatic Suilven has a long
approach but is well worth the effort.
Scrambling is only required for the
eastern summit.**

Start from the south end of Lochinver.
About 40m north of the turning for
Inverkirkaig, a single-track road signposted
for Ledmore climbs east (GR094223). After
1.5km, this becomes a private track and
winds through the estate of Glencanisp
Lodge, exiting by a gate. Follow the track
for 300m beyond the gate and, rather than

descending to the loch, pass through a gate
on the left to head ESE on a path overlooking
the Abhainn na Clach Airigh. In fine weather,
the mesmerising sight of Caisteal Liath,
Suilven's westernmost summit, dominates
the approach. After 5km, cross a bridge to
the south bank and continue along the track
for a further 400m. A path trends southwest
over the moor: this may be difficult to locate
and follow at first, but definition improves.
The path passes between two small lochans,
Loch na Barrack and Loch a'Choire Dhuibh,
and on towards the bealach between
Suilven's two main towers. Climb steeply up
over scree and broken boulders to reach
Bealach Mór and its crazy wall. The main
summit of Caisteal Liath is an easy climb
WNW (GR153184) (4h). Return to the

◀ Suilven from Glencanisp Lodge

bealach. [Detour: to climb the east summit, walk ESE over a small tower before climbing Meall Meadhonach, keeping slightly to the south side. This involves two tricky sections of scrambling that also have to be descended. Return to Bealach Mór (add 1h).] Descend steeply over scree on the southwest side to the boggy expanse below. A vague path leads westwards across the moor to come close to Fionn Loch at Coire Mór. Pick up a good path here and follow it northwest for just over 1km. At the point where the path turns abruptly southeast beside the narrow westernmost inlet of Fionn Loch, leave it to skirt around Loch Uidh na Ceardaich on its northern side, crossing a small burn. At the west end of the loch, climb west over a knoll to enter a

hidden gorge with a long wall that runs through the middle. Follow this to Loch a'Ghlinne Sgoilte. Pass the loch on the northern shore to follow the burn from the far end. This soon leads to the start of a good path at Loch Bad na Múirichinn. Follow the east side of the loch over a burn: at this point the path disappears, but continue around a knoll with some low walls to rejoin the path. This leads along the north shore and, from the foot of the loch, follows a ravine northwest. Pass through a set of sheep pens and cross the field to join the road. Turn right to walk in the direction of Lochinver (7h40). [Variant: the last 1km of road walking can be avoided by entering Culag Forest, accessed just after the steep hairpins at GR093214.]

Sutherland and Caithness in the Far North are quite unlike the rest of the Highlands. The coastline is famed for its quiet beaches, sea stacks, and hidden inlets and caves. In contrast, bog dominates the hinterland and much of the area is uninhabited.

On the northwest tip, near Durness, there are some spectacular peaks, high craggy domes and mountain chains laden with scree. The hills continue to the south and east along Long Shin, but then disappear before re-emerging near the North Sea as a different, smaller range.

In this section, the circuits of Ben Stack and Arkle start near Loch Laxford. A route over the sprawling crest of Foinaven begins closer to Durness. The unusual rocky tors of Ben Loyal are within walking distance of Tongue, and this village also provides a good base for climbing Ben Hope. The tiny village of Crask, between Lairg and Tongue, is the start point for a route around Ben Klibreck. The shores of Loch Merkland to the west mark the start of a route on Ben Hee. A long traverse of Morven and Scaraben sets out from near Dunbeath on the North Sea coast.

The Far North

1 **Ben Stack and the thousand lochans**   80
Half-day route over a classic whaleback peak with good approach
paths and one steep climb to the top

2 **The Screes of Arkle**   82
Rough ground, oceans of scree and a rocky ascent make for a
challenging route

3 **Foinaven**   84
Arduous but entertaining circuit of the multi-topped Foinaven
with some steep sections of ascent and descent, and scree aplenty

4 **Ben Hope and the Moine Thrust**   86
Challenging circuit of Ben Hope, negotiating some tricky terrain
and returning over moorland on an old path

5 **Crags and tors of Ben Loyal**   88
Exciting walk over multiple rocky tops with a moorland approach
and optional scrambling on descent

6 **Ben Klibreck over Strathnaver**   90
Long walk over an isolated mountain with easy grassy ridges but
few paths, starting out from Crask

7 **Ben Hee and the Robber's Pass**   92
Quiet peak far from any town or village. This route climbs two
tops and returns by a good track

8 **Morven and Scaraben**   94
Long mostly off-path route over two well-known peaks with
interesting rock formations and quiet moorland

Ben Stack and the thousand lochans

Ben Stack (721m)

Walk time 3h40 Height gain 700m
Distance 9km
OS Maps Landranger 9 and 15

**A steep climb up a prominent peak
with a spectacular panorama over the
Sutherland coast and islands.**

Start by a telephone box in Achfary, 10km
southeast of Laxford Bridge (GR293396).
A track leads westwards past a set of old
but well-preserved cottages to reach a gate
into the forest. Beyond the gate, the track
climbs gently WNW, providing occasional
glimpses of the chasm through which the
Allt Achadh Fairidh flows. The track leaves
the forest, but trees continue on the south
side before eventually thinning out. Soon
after, the track deteriorates to a path. About
1km after the last trees (and level with a
waterfall on the opposite bank), leave the
path and climb north by a burn. Follow this
over steep heather ramps and terraces
to its source in flatter ground. Continue
steeply north over uneven terrain to the
rounded west ridge of Ben Stack, where
rock fins and small patches of scree can
be bypassed or scrambled to reach the

summit (GR269423) (2h40). Follow the narrow ridge ESE to the trig point and mast, dropping quite suddenly southeast to a small level area. Climb a knoll before descending the broad and uneven flanks of Leathad na Stioma, aiming for Loch More. A boggy track starts close to the corner of the forest, wending its way through moorland to reach the road. Walk south to the start (3h40).

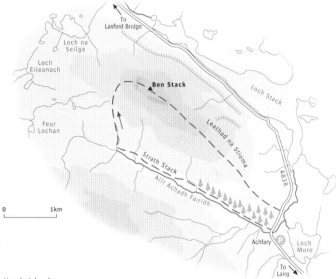

Handa Island

This tiny island was once inhabited by twelve families who lived on potatoes, fish and seabirds and appointed their own parliament and the oldest widow in the community as their queen. The 1846 famine forced the islanders to leave for the mainland and then Cape Breton and, except for puffins, fulmars, shags, terns, gulls, kittiwakes, auks, arctic skuas, a Scottish Wildlife Trust warden and 100,000 resident guillemots, it remains uninhabited. Visitors can access the island by boat from Tarbet.

◀ Looking west from Ben Stack

The Screes of Arkle

Arkle ⊙ (787m)

Walk time 6h Height gain 800m
Distance 15km OS Map Landranger 9

A half-day route over a crumbling mountain. The ascent over scree can be hard going but is rewarded with views over Foinaven.

Start from the A838 at the turn-off for Lochstack Lodge (GR268436). (Park here or 400m northwest.) Walk down the road towards the lodge, and turn right just after the bridge to follow a good grassy track which trends first east and then northeast across moorland. The track turns 90 degrees to bear northwest just after Loch an Nighe

Leathaid: follow it for a further 1km as it begins to rise, and arc eastwards. At a suitable point, leave the track and bear ESE over folding terrain with crags and grassy terraces to reach the base of the screes on the apex of the vague northwest spur of Sàil Mhór. The jagged scree is not too steep, and runnels of grass and boulders can be followed to make the journey easier.

As height is gained, dozens of lochans come into view. The ground eases shortly before the summit (GR302462) (3h20). Continue southwards over interesting sandstone blocks: the ridge gives views over the vast scree slopes of Arkle and Foinaven. A smaller top is ascended

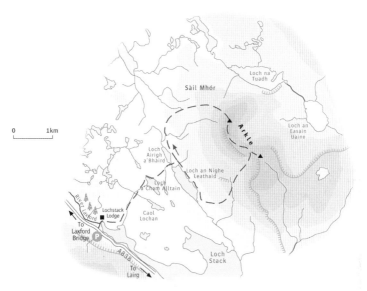

before dropping to a prominent bealach (GR307455). Climb the south summit and return to the bealach. Drop down the south side to find a good path which follows a burn steeply until it passes the lowest band of cliffs. Now bear westwards to Loch an Nighe Leathaid, and hug the east side of the loch to reach the original track. This leads directly to the start point (6h).

Crofting

Contrary to popular belief, crofting is not an ancient way of life and only developed in the early 19th century as landlords sought to make greater profits from their tenants. Crofts were plots of land, usually in coastal areas, which were not sufficient for their occupants to make a living from. This usually meant that they had to work cheaply for their landlord in the booming kelp industry to survive. When that collapsed in the 1820s, rents rose and more grazing land was cleared for sheep. The Crofters' Act of 1886 eventually addressed the problem of security of tenure and fair rent, but by then thousands had been forced from their ancient homelands and their way of life lost.

◀ Loch Stack and Arkle in cloud

Foinaven

Foinaven: **Ceann Garbh** (902m),
Ganu Mór ⓒ (914m) and other tops

Walk time 8h Height gain 1000m
Distance 23km OS Map Landranger 9

**The many spurs and tops of Foinaven
make for exciting climbing, whichever
route you take. This circuit involves
some tricky sections in descent, and is
serious in winter.**

Start at Gualin House, midway between
Durness and Laxford Bridge (GR308567).
(Two parking areas are located a few
hundred metres east of the house on the

A838.) From the west side of the estate
entrance, walk south between lochans and
over a vast bog, aiming for the bulk of
Ceann Garbh. After some effort, the ground
rises to gain a set of steep red crags on the
north face of this peak. Pass the crags on
the left to follow a vague ridge straight up
to a shoulder (easier than it looks from
below) where the angle eases. This leads
SSE to Ceann Garbh with its huge cliffs to
the east, the first of many tops (GR314515)
(3h20). Follow the ridge south, dropping
gradually, before climbing the vast scree
skirt of Ganu Mór, the true summit of

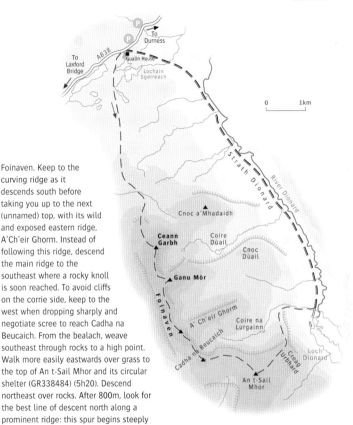

Foinaven. Keep to the curving ridge as it descends south before taking you up to the next (unnamed) top, with its wild and exposed eastern ridge, A'Ch'eir Ghorm. Instead of following this ridge, descend the main ridge to the southeast where a rocky knoll is soon reached. To avoid cliffs on the corrie side, keep to the west when dropping sharply and negotiate scree to reach Cadha na Beucaich. From the bealach, weave southeast through rocks to a high point. Walk more easily eastwards over grass to the top of An t-Sail Mhor and its circular shelter (GR338484) (5h20). Descend northeast over rocks. After 800m, look for the best line of descent north along a prominent ridge: this spur begins steeply and awkwardly with the occasional rock step. Lower down, as you approach the burn which flows through Coire na Lurgainn, drop east into Strath Dionard to join a track. [Variant: if the northerly descent from An t-Sail Mhor feels too difficult, return to the

summit and walk gently south for about 2km to Bealach Horn. Drop east to An Dubh-loch on a grassy path, and continue north to Loch Dionard to find the north end of the track (add 1h20).] Bear northwards on the track for 8km to Gualin House (8h).

◄ Looking south along the ridge of Foinaven from Ganu Mór

Ben Hope and the Moine Thrust

Ben Hope (927m)

Walk time 6h Height gain 900m
Distance 15km OS Map Landranger 9

Ben Hope is a mountain with many faces: steep cliffs to the west, deep corries to the east and an expanse of gently sloping moorland to the south.

Start from the car park by a large barn on the road between Hope and Altnaharra (GR463476). Take the path which climbs steeply northeast by a burn. Higher up, this passes on the south side of some cliffs with notable quartz veins, and then continues to climb east to flatter ground: now head NNE for 2km to the summit of Ben Hope (GR477501) (2h40). From the trig point, descend eastwards over steep boulders camouflaged by moss. The slope relents along the broad central ridge between the two eastern corries, inhospitable amphitheatres of rock and scree. As you approach the twin lochs below, one higher than the other, the terrain becomes complex and uneven: head towards the south end of Loch na Seilg, the lower loch. Follow the shoreline to the north end and descend lush slopes, keeping west of the An Garbh-allt. After about 2km, look out for an old grassy track which cuts across from east to west (it is easy to miss). This is the Moine Path, which leads southwest over quiet moorland and gains the road by Loch Hope. Follow the road south to the start (6h).

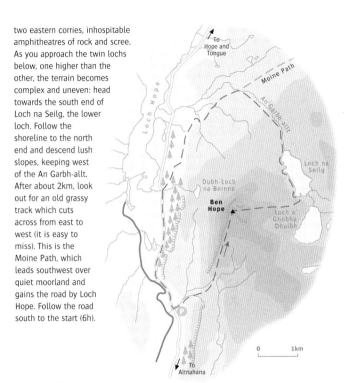

The Moine Thrust

The northwest of Scotland contains some of the best exposed geology in Britain. Victorian interest in geology brought about the discovery of the Moine Thrust Belt. This extends from Skye to Loch Eriboll, and has helped in the understanding of how mountains are created as well as in developing scientific methods of study. The belt is a low-angled fault and is characterised by the displacement of younger rocks by older strata.

◄ Ben Hope and Loch Hope

Crags and tors of Ben Loyal

Ben Loyal: An Caisteal Ⓒ(764m)

Walk time 6h20 Height gain 800m
Distance 16km OS Map Landranger 10

**A multi-topped granite mountain in a
remote part of the country. The descent
is tricky, but scrambling can be avoided.
Dogs are not allowed on this walk.**

Start at a turning for Ribigill, 2km south
of Tongue on the road to Kinloch
(GR584548). (Park just before the gate or in
Tongue.) Follow the track south, and take
the turning to Ribigill Farm after 800m.
A good track keeps east of the farm
buildings and crosses the farmland. It

continues as a path across the moor, and
fords the Allt Lòn Malmsgaig within sight of
the croft at Cunside. Climb steadily
southwards by a narrow path towards the
Bealach Clais nan Ceap. Bear southwest
before you come to the bealach, and climb
steeply west over heather to gain the top of
Sgòr Chaonasaid. The hardest part of the
day's climbing is over, and the route now
undulates over the great crag-ringed tops of
the Ben Loyal massif. Continue to the cliffs
of Sgòr a'Bhatain and then south to climb
An Caisteal. This is a well-named fortress
with easy access only from the north to its
summit (GR577489) (3h20). Double back

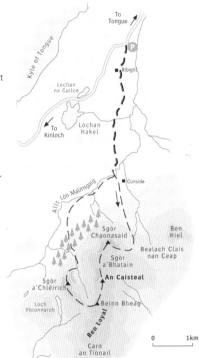

onto easy ground to avoid the cliffs, and contour on the corrie side towards Beinn Bheag. This rounded hill can be climbed directly or avoided on the west by an exciting path high above the corrie. Descend west to a bealach before tackling the last short climb to the top of Sgòr a'Chléirich. There are steep cliffs on all sides of this peak, and the north ridge provides an entertaining but tricky descent. The first section begins with a rocky corner, after which other difficult parts can be more easily negotiated on the west side of the ridge. Lower down, drop northeast to reach and cross the burn flowing from the corrie. [Variant: to avoid the descent from Sgòr a'Chléirich, return to the bealach with Beinn Bheag and drop easily north into the corrie.] Descend to the trees, and then directly to the moorland below. Bear northeast towards Cunside. Cross the Allt Lòn Malmsgaig, and follow the path and track back to Ribigill and the start (6h20).

The Prince's Lost Gold

In 1746, carrying over £13,000 in gold coin to fund Bonnie Prince Charlie's ill-fated rising, the ship *Hazard* tried to hide from a pursuing Royal Navy frigate in the Kyle of Tongue. The Jacobite crew threw the gold into the loch before being captured, and it was recovered by government forces. The Prince sent 1500 of his men north to try to regain the booty, but they were captured or killed en route. It is a matter of some debate as to whether those men would have made a difference at the later battle on Culloden Moor.

◂ Ben Loyal from the north

Ben Klibreck over Strathnaver

Ben Klibreck: Meall nan Con ⑩(962m)

Walk time 8h Height gain 1000m
Distance 22km OS Map Landranger 16

**A long route up an elegant peak
and over rounded hills, returning by
a hidden glen to Crask.**

Start at the Crask Inn (GR524247). Walk
200m south along the road to a gate, just
before a bridge. Go through the gate, and
follow a footpath east along the River Tirry
with forest on the far bank. The path begins
to rise as it parts company with the burn:
continue until level with a second

plantation and a stone circle on the
right. Leave the path here, and climb
north up slopes which gently ease towards
a knoll with a cairn. Follow the remains
of old fencing northwards: the terrain
begins to steepen but levels out below
Creag an Lochain. Climb northeast to the
top which reveals more high ground
beyond (GR576280) (3h). Descend easily
north along the ridge to reach A'Chioch and
then bear eastwards to climb steeply over
rocks to Meall nan Con, the summit of
Ben Klibreck (GR585299) (4h40). Drop
south from the trig point along a grassy

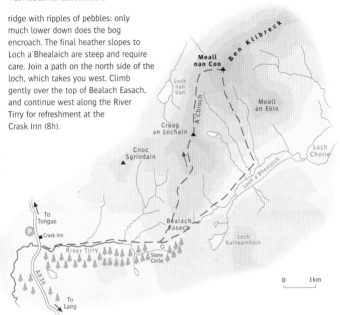

◀ Ben Klibreck from above Altnaharra

ridge with ripples of pebbles: only much lower down does the bog encroach. The final heather slopes to Loch a'Bhealaich are steep and require care. Join a path on the north side of the loch, which takes you west. Climb gently over the top of Bealach Easach, and continue west along the River Tirry for refreshment at the Crask Inn (8h).

The Strathnaver Clearances

Before the Clearances, the fertile northern shore of Loch Naver in the shadow of Ben Klibreck was busy with small townships. Rhifail, Skail, Syre, Grummore, Grumbeg and Achness were home to dozens of families until Patrick Sellar, a factor for Lord and Lady Stafford, carried out the most ruthless of evictions and burnt the houses and mills. Sellar was brought to trial in Inverness for the culpable homicide of two elderly residents, but was acquitted by a jury of affluent merchants and landowners. The people of the strath were displaced by sheep and forced to the barren coastlands of Strathy Point, while Sellar retired to the estate given to him by his grateful employers.

Ben Hee and the Robber's Pass

Ben Hee Ⓖ (873m)

Walk time 5h40 **Height gain** 900m
Distance 15km **OS Map** Landranger 16

**A remote and little visited mountain
surrounded by the peaks and wild
moorland of Sutherland. The return
follows the secluded Robber's Pass.**

Start from West Merkland at the north
end of Loch Merkland (GR384329). (Park
with care or 800m northwest.) Follow the
gravel track northwards above the Allt
nan Albannach for 1.5km until it meets
with the Allt Coir' a'Chruiteir. A small path
follows this burn east on its south bank:
it is hard to pick up but becomes obvious
a little higher where the glen narrows.
Higher still, where the glen opens up to a
corrie, the path becomes faint. Continue
east over sandstone boulders and grass to
the summit of Ben Hee (GR426339) (2h40).
Follow the ridge northwest around the

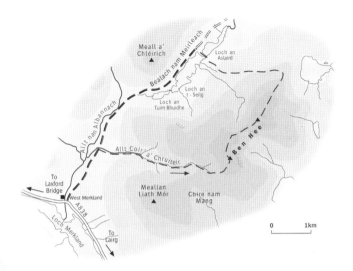

eastern corrie for 250m, and then northeast down to a bealach. Continue to make your way around the corrie, and climb northeast past some crags on the right and then on towards the wide expanse of a second top. The scree slopes on the northwest side are awkward and, to descend, it is preferable to continue northeast for 1km where it becomes easier to turn westwards. Aim for a gap between Loch an Aslaird and Loch an t-Seilg. A path crosses the burn between the lochs by stepping stones to reach a track at Bealach nam Meirleach, the Robber's Pass. Follow the track southwest to the start point (5h40).

Hill lochs

The clean, well-oxygenated hill lochs of Sutherland are home to the native trout of Scotland, *Salmo trutta*, which feed almost entirely on tiny aquatic invertebrates and on flies blown from the surrounding land. In deeper lochs some trout develop the ferox habit of feeding on other fish, especially arctic charr, and can grow very large. There are two broad types of trout – freshwater brown trout and sea-running migrants – but also intermediates between these, known as slob trout. Like salmon, all of these fish possess the instinct to return to their natal areas to spawn in early winter.

◀ Ben Hee from Strath More

Morven and Scaraben

Scaraben (626m), **Morven** (706m)

Walk time 8h20 Height gain 1200m
Distance 23km OS Map Landranger 17

A long walk over moorland which climbs two popular peaks of the northeast.

Start by a telephone box and bridge at the end of the public road at Braemore (GR073304). (Limited parking here.) Cross the bridge, and immediately turn left to double back east on a farm track beside the Berriedale Water. Pass a suspension footbridge and go through a gate, after which the track loses definition. Further downriver, the path starts to climb a little. When the route loses height at the old telegraph posts, leave the path and bear southwest up clumpy heather and grass. Gain the east ridge of Scaraben, and follow the fenceposts to the east summit. Drop a short way to walk to the main summit (GR066268) (2h40). Descend on the west to another bealach, and then climb to the subsidiary top of Sròn Gharbh. Leave by the north ridge, and drop west into a flat and secluded basin before climbing northwest to the top of Smean and its pebble-encrusted tors. Continue to Càrn Mór, and descend

west to reach the bottom of the steep and even slopes of Morven. Climb west up heather or large and stable scree. This eventually leads to a buttress which is easily breached: it is just a short way to the summit (GR004285) (6h). Descend by the steep-sided western arête. Lower down the ridge blurs, so drop steeply northwards to gentler ground. Bear eastwards over heather from here, heading for the river and the prominent stack of Maiden Pap. When you reach the croft at Corrichoich, follow the grassy track which runs eastwards alongside a plantation, past the farm at Braeval and back to the start point (8h20).

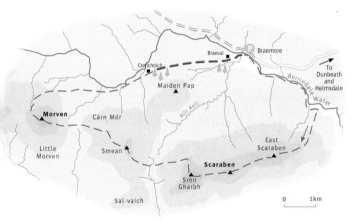

The Duke

During the Clearances, Helmsdale was an experiment instigated by Lord Stafford, 1st Duke of Sutherland, to turn his tenants into herring fishermen as an alternative to emigration. When the Duke died in 1833 money was raised, much of it from the tenants he evicted, to build a massive statue of him wearing a red sandstone toga on Beinn a'Bhragaidh overlooking Golspie. Despite the best efforts of pressure groups who would like to see this monument brought down, the Duke still stands, looking out to the sea where he sent his tenants as emigrants or herring fishermen.

◀ Maiden Pap and Morven from Braemore

Index

Á Mhaighdean (967m)	34
A'Chailleach (997m)	16
Am Faochagach (953m)	14
An Caisteal (764m)	88
An Coileachan (923m)	10
An Ruadh-stac (892m)	56
An Teallach	24
Arkle (787m)	82
Baosbheinn (875m)	32
Beinn Alligin	48
Beinn a'Chlaidheimh (916m)	26
Beinn an Eòin (855m)	32
Beinn Bhàn (895m)	54
Beinn Damh (903m)	52
Beinn Dearg (Loch Droma) (1084m)	14
Beinn Dearg (Torridon) (914m)	50
Beinn Dearg Bheag (820m)	30
Beinn Dearg Mór (910m)	30
Beinn Eighe	42,44
Beinn Ghobhlach (635m)	28
Beinn Liath Mhòr (926m)	58
Beinn Liath Mhòr Fannaich (954m)	10
Beinn nan Caorach (649m)	64
Beinn Tarsuinn (937m)	26
Ben Hee (873m)	92
Ben Hope (927m)	86
Ben Klibreck	90
Ben Loyal	88
Ben Mór Coigach (743m)	64
Ben More Assynt (998m)	70
Ben Stack (721m)	80
Ben Wyvis	8
Bidein a'Ghlas Thuill (1062m)	24
Cairn Conmheall (541m)	64
Caisteal Liath (731m)	76
Carn Bàn (845m)	20
Ceann Garbh (902m)	84
Còinneach Mhór (976m)	44
Cona' Mheall (978m)	14
Conival (987m)	70
Creag-mheall Mór (628m)	30
Cùl Beag (769m)	66
Cùl Mór (849m)	68
Eididh nan Clach Geala (927m)	18
Fionn Bheinn (933m)	12
Foinaven	84
Fuar Tholl (907m)	58
Ganu Mór (914m)	84
Garbh Choireachan (733m)	64
Glas Bheinn (776m)	74
Glas Leathad Mór (1046m)	8
Liathach	46
Maol Chean-dearg (933m)	56
Meall a'Chrasgaidh (934m)	10
Meall a'Ghiubhais (887m)	36
Meall Gorm (949m)	10
Meall Meadhonach (723m)	76
Meall nan Ceapraichean (977m)	18
Meall nan Con (962m)	90
Morven (706m)	94
Mullach an Rathain (1023m)	46
Mullach Coire Mhic Fhearchair (1018m)	26
Na Rathanan (866m)	48
Quinag	72
Ruadh-stac Beag (896m)	42
Ruadh Stac Mór (Letterewe) (918m)	34
Ruadh-stac Mór (Beinn Eighe) (1010m)	44
Sàil Gharbh (808m)	72
Sàil Gorm (776m)	72
Sàil Liath (954m)	24
Scaraben (626m)	94
Seana Bhraigh (927m)	20
Sgorr Ruadh (962m)	58
Sgùrr an Fhidhleir (703m)	64
Sgùrr an Tuill Bhàin (934m)	38
Sgùrr Bàn (Dundonnell) (989m)	26
Sgùrr Bàn (Beinn Eighe) (970m)	42
Sgùrr Breac (999m)	16
Sgùrr Dubh (738m)	38
Sgùrr Fiòna (1060m)	24
Sgùrr Mhór (Beinn Alligin) (986m)	48
Sgùrr Mór (Fannichs) (1110m)	10
Sgurr nan Clach Geala (1093m)	10
Sgurr nan Each (923m)	10
Sgurr nan Fhir Duibhe (963m)	42
Slioch (981m)	38
Speicein Còinnich (717m)	64
Spidean a Choire Léith (1055m)	46
Spidean Còinich (764m)	72
Spidean Coire nan Clach (993m)	42,44
Stac Pollaidh (613m)	62
Stùc a'Choire Dhuibh Bhig (915m)	46
Suilven	76
Tom a'Chòinnich (953m)	8
Tom na Gruagaich (922m)	48

Munros are mountains in Scotland above 914m (3000ft). (Named after Sir Hugh Munro who compiled the first list in 1891.)

Corbetts are peaks between 762m and 914m (2500ft and 3000ft) which have a drop of at least 152m (500ft) on all sides. (Named after John Corbett who drew up the list and made the first ascent.)